The
LIFE AND PRIVATE HISTORY
of
EMILY JANE BRONTË

By
ROMER WILSON

With Ten Illustrations

NEW YORK
ALBERT AND CHARLES BONI
1928

Kessinger Publishing's Rare Reprints
Thousands of Scarce and Hard-to-Find Books!

We kindly invite you to view our extensive catalog list at:
http://www.kessinger.net

Drawing by Anne Gliddon, Nov., 1840   *National Portrait Gallery, London*

GEORGE HENRY LEWES

"The aspect of Lewes's face almost moves me to tears; it is so wonderfully like Emily, her eyes, her features, the very nose, the somewhat prominent mouth, the forehead, even, at moments, the expression."—*Charlotte Brontë to Ellen Nussey.*

Printed in the United States of America

Contents

vii

CONTENTS

Illustrations

References and Commentaries

THIS life of Emily Jane Brontë is based chiefly upon the internal evidence of her poems, most of which Mr. C. W. Hatfield has now arranged in chronological order.

I read these with the letters of Charlotte Brontë, which I supplemented with extreme caution by the novels and poems of the family.

The famous prefaces of Charlotte Brontë written to her sisters' works for publication contain many errors, not only errors of date. It is safe to say that almost all dates, ages, or seasons referred to by Charlotte in recollection are incorrect. For instance, Charlotte says Emily was twenty when she went to Brussels. Emily became twenty-four during the nine months she passed there. Moreover almost no statement of hers in reminiscence is untainted by what Charlotte *wished had been the case*. The wish was very often father, not only of her thoughts, but of her memories. Her logic and her ability to suit the past event, and even the present, to the occasion, were feminine faults in her, inconvenient to biographers of her family.

In conclusion, this life does not purport to be a Last Word upon Emily Jane Brontë's history. I know Emily herself now. I do not know all the events by any means which befell her, nor absolutely the order of those I have recorded. I know the main lines of her character, the most important part of her history. Time will probably clear up many matters. I do not care how erroneous my statements of fact are, provided these statements draw forth clear and correct evidence from secret hiding-places. I have been as accurate as possible. A thin stream of inaccuracies weakly diluted with truth has been the source I have had to rely upon for the incidents of Emily's career.

I have to thank Thomas J. Wise, Esq., for most kindly permitting me to inspect the original manuscript of *The Wanderer*, dated Bradford, 1838, by Emily Jane Brontë; C. W. Hatfield, Esq., for his voluntary and invaluable assistance in dating many poems, in correcting published texts by manuscript readings in his possession, in furnishing me with the photograph of Emily's manuscript reproduced in the present volume, and in furnishing much other information; Davidson Cook, Esq., for a photograph of MS. of *No Coward Soul Is Mine* and for permission to quote textual readings from his article in *The Nineteenth Century and After* for August, 1926; the Executors of the late Clement Shorter, Esq., for permission to quote from *The Brontës: Life and Letters* by Clement Shorter, Dodd, Mead and Company, 1908, and *The Complete Poems of Emily Jane Brontë*, edited by Clement Shorter, and arranged and collated with bibliography and notes by C. W. Hatfield, George H. Doran Company, and Doubleday, Doran and Company, 1923; Messrs. Dodd, Mead and Company for confirming this permission; Mr. Jack Hewer, Esq., for his offer of all his Brontë etchings, only two of which

I could use owing to limited space; Messrs. Arthur Greatorex, Ltd., 14 Grafton St., Bond St., London, the original publishers and owners of the copyright of Mr. Hewer's etchings; The National Portrait Gallery, London, for the use of four reproductions from portraits in that collection; and to Mr. John Grant for permission to reprint The Famous Street and Haworth Church from *Lives of the Brontës*.

References:

"David," Michelangelo.

"Paradise Lost," Milton.

"Une Saison en Enfer," Rimbaud.

"Moby Dick," Melville.

Complete Works of Nietzsche and Dostoevsky.

"Parsifal," Wagner.

Later works of Beethoven.

"The Plumed Serpent," D. H. Lawrence.

"Ulysses," James Joyce.

"Revolt in the Desert," T. E. Lawrence, etc.

Commentaries:

"Napoleon," Emil Ludwig.

"The New Criterion," edited by T. S. Eliot.

"The Enemy," edited by Wyndham Lewis, etc.

INTRODUCTION TO HAWORTH

A JOURNEY FROM TO-DAY

"What is that smoke that ever still
Comes rolling down that dark brown hill?"
Emily Jane Brontë

WEST and north and south the moors hang above the West Riding of Yorkshire. They rise up bleak and black and brooding, a thousand feet, two thousand feet above the valleys. Empty and silent, without trees or lakes, without wide rivers, without grand impressive mountains, they roll away from this world. Though not above forty miles by East and West, and one hundred and fifty by North and South, these moors contrive to be virgin, desolate and immune. Lancaster and Manchester send forth smoke on the one side of them, Sheffield, Leeds and Bradford, on the other, so that on still days, the smoke of the cities hangs in a gloom under the sky; and on such a day colours have an aniline brilliance, the green moss is livid, a white flower stares like a blind white star out of the sombre afternoon, and the cry of the peewits as they circle low above the heather, is shrill, metallic, ominous.

On such a day I stood in the little garden of my lodgings at Hathersage in Derbyshire, down in the Hope

1

Valley where Jane Eyre took refuge from Rochester. I stared up at the long black crest of rock a thousand feet above me, that long black ramp of rock against the sky. The phlox and sweet-williams in the garden stared wide-eyed at me. There was not a breath of air.

I went out into the grey stone town and up the stony road, up and up from Derbyshire, into Yorkshire over Stannidge Edge. "Go back! Go back! Go back!" the grouse called through the gloomy afternoon. I pushed along the Roman Road past Stannidge Pole thinking of Cæsar's Wars, past Redmires Dam, and tried a woeful short cut through bog and peat and rabbit-holes and knee-deep heather to the Manchester Road. "Go back! Go back!" the eternal cry of the grouse rang across the dark brown endless moor. At last I struck the blue shining Manchester Road, but soon was off on a rough turf and metal lane to Strines.

At Strines there is nothing but an ancient Inn. The Manners' peacock is carved in stone over the door. There is a stone roof to the stone house, stone mullions at the narrow windows and stone floors within doors. The Inn is low and long and half sunk down under the lea of the moor. There will be ham and eggs for high tea, and though it is July, a roasting fire burns red in the old-fashioned sitting-room.

I sit down and rest beside the huge fire in the musty old room. From somewhere in the depths of the house comes a smell of frying ham. I cannot rest long. Curiosity impels me to get up and look at the engraving of

2

Queen Victoria's wedding above the silk-bosomed piano. "God Save Our Gracious Queen!" She was almost precisely of an age with Emily Brontë, and like her, had seen three kings as they say, for she also was born in the reign of George the Third. Well! Well! Victoria would not have liked Emily Jane, though she herself was wild enough in the intoxication of early accession to a throne.

Tea delays to appear. I cannot remain still. There is a restlessness in this place and this scene of other days has set me dreaming. If I were King! I look out of the window at the garden before the house until I become conscious that there is no garden, but only a patch of short green turf, a few stone flags, some rickety Sunday School benches and a trestle table under the lean sycamores. Behind the sycamores, the endless uprising of the moors.

I sigh and wander out of doors to examine the beautiful old door again. It is like the door of *Wuthering Heights*. There certainly is an unrest in this high-pitched spot. The door though beautiful is strange. Memory hangs about it, memory of evil words long spoken and evil deeds long done, and of dead days in winter when not a soul comes to disturb this silence, of the howling of autumn wind when the blackened leaves of the sycamores whirl into corners and leap against the house.

I am called to tea.

A woman puts a great jug of coffee and a fine large dish of ham before me.

3

"Shall you be staying?" she asks.
"One night. Lonely here!"
"Aye, 'tis that!"
"In winter."
"Fit to brak yer 'eart!"
"Heartbreak House," I say.
"Aye, 'tis that an' all."
They still talk the old talk of Joseph in *Wuthering Heights*. Between one thing and another, come night, I have journeyed back a hundred years.

Next day I push north along the moorland road past Agden and Broomhead Hall. The moors roll up and up to the west. Eastward the hills descend into the valleys. Agden moor! I was joint-owner once of Agden moor. Vain thought! who can own a moor? I am alone on the sandy moor road, alone with myself and my dreams. "Go back! Go back!" cry the grouse, but with a sense of opposition I go on. A low wind whispers in the fine silvery grass. "Ssh! ssh! ssh!" "Go back! Go back!" The heather is pink with little beads of buds, millions of little beads of buds. Grass and heather quiver in the wind. Millions of quivering grass blades and quivering little beads as far as eye can see. I am alone in a vast quivering silence, for it is silent, though the wind whispers and the grouse cry; it is silent and still and far off.

Foreigners rarely wander here, but I, who belong to these parts, like to be alone on the moors, for I know myself then and walk with myself hand in hand. I am a hero, my own hero, the man whom no one knows.

THE FAMOUS STREET UP TO THE CHURCH AND PARSONAGE
Reproduced by permission of Mr. John Grant from "Lives of the Brontës"

Nor do I care now that no one knows him. Alone on the moor I care for neither God nor man, but only for myself, who have always been I from the time when other folk called me a child, and before that, always, back to the beginning, if eternity ever began.

But to Haworth, whither I am bound, it is a long roundabout way from here by the hills; and since my heroic soul is lodged in flesh and bone and too much exaltation disagrees with my stomach, I descend to Penistone where dirt is consummate, and take the train through Huddersfield, Halifax, and Bradford to Keighley. In the train I suffer a sad reaction; disappointment, self-pity and a sense of loss. At Keighley, half ashamed of past ecstasy, half angry with machinery and men, I persuade my feet to walk the four grim miles to Haworth which Charlotte and Emily Brontë so often tramped for the sake of a new book from the lending library. It is a hideous and dirty walk. The July heat smells of coal; grit blows up on the July wind. The footpath is purple with cinders and the hills are awful. God has forsaken this grim road if ever He dwelt in the locality at all.

At last I attain the Black Bull at the top of Haworth hill. Yonder is the church and the parsonage. Graves lie everywhere. I think of Sedan and Waterloo. Here are the graves of people the moors have killed in battle with the towns. Behind all the eternal moors rise darkly. People should not live here on this strange frontier.

. . . .

Haworth has earned a black reputation. Black it is

5

in feature, black as an old woodcut, the houses, the church, the scraggy trees, the crows.

In spring a very green green peers between, and creeps and hangs upon the black; in winter, green and black are largely blotted out with white. But spring, summer or winter, Haworth remains a gloomy woodcut. There is nothing exceptional about Haworth. The town, weather-blackened and sooty, had not then and has not now, a character uncommon to its neighbours. The public-houses, the mournful Methodist chapels, the stunted stone-roofed dwellings with three windows and a narrow door, crowd up the narrow steep streets. In our time dirty brick, blue slate, yellow-grained bow-windows, a "garridge" with glaring red and yellow petrol advertisements, cling parasitically about the crooked streets. Even so, Haworth differs little from Hebdenbridge or Bolsterstone or many another weather-blackened, sooty spot; nor has it changed essentially these hundred years in outward feature or inward pride, nor lost its robust contempt for the outer world, nor for that most alien, uncaring and unconscious South. It is bred in our bone to pity and despise the South of England, Londoners and all such trash. I own it for a fault and for a virtue, and confess that in my heart of hearts jealousy and genuine contempt for what I cannot know and do not try to understand dwell side by side.

Though it is hot in Haworth to-day, that is an accident. There is no end to winter up here. It can snow with as good a heart in September or May as in any month between. It can freeze in June and reek with

6

fog in August and the rain is not far distant at any time. Sometimes there is a gentle wind, or a bright joyous cloud-chasing wind makes the heart glad; sometimes there settles a dead brooding calm in summer, or a cold black stillness in winter, but often the gale tears and roars down over the moors, or teasing gusts sweep up from the face of the earth to drive and torment us.

The houses are thick and stolid, windproof and frequently damp, but the parsonage is a good house, though all the living rooms overlook the churchyard. It was originally entirely built of stone, save the window frames and the floors of the upper rooms. Roof, stairs, parlour floor, backyard, garden walks, everything that in a gentler climate might be made of brick or wood or slate, was stone here once, and is chiefly stone still. In the old days there were three excellent rooms downstairs, the kitchen, the parlour and the study. Above stairs there were four bedrooms, and a bit of a den with a window filling one end and a door the other. There was no sanitation. The house was as primitive in this respect as most houses of its day. Nay, many a country spot is no better now. All the garbage of the household was thrown into an ashpit or upon a dung heap. This horrible accumulation usually leaked into the soil, probably into the well, a few feet away. The graveyard as in most northern villages was raised above the houses, and it drained also into all the nearby wells. The dead lie above the living in our villages.

Haworth [1] was plagued with fever. "Low Fever," a typhoid infection, continuously perambulated the town, and in wet weather there were many funerals. But for years, though urged to it, the local landowners paid no heed to warning or catastrophe; corpses rotted, ashpits leaked, the wells brought death from the dead to the living because no man cared "to put his money underground." "Low Fever" and "English Cholera" are now things of the past. Motor buses run to Haworth, and there is a railway in the Bottom, as we call the valley. Yet the Parsonage and the Black Bull still stand, the wind still blows, and the folk still talk the outlandish lingo of their fathers; and in spite of the board-school, cinema and garage, act as they acted then, and for the most part live the same hard passionate lives.

[1] In the first half of last century the death rate in Bradford reached as high as 38 per 100 per annum. At a moderate estimate at least 150 persons perished every year in Haworth with its population of under 6,000.

8

I

A SELF-MADE GENTLEMAN

"Nature never intended [him] to make a very good husband, especially to a quiet wife."
Shirley. Charlotte Brontë

"Suspected slights of his authority nearly threw him into fits."
Wuthering Heights. Emily Jane Brontë

ONE spring day in 1820, the year after George III died mad, there came to Haworth Parsonage a tall strong Irishman accompanied by a frail wife and six very small children, as young as six children can possibly be who are none of them twins.

This man, the Reverend Patrick Brontë, was the new vicar. He had left the only place on earth where he was really happy. There were charming neighbours at Thornton, the curacy he had just vacated, of whom he was genuinely fond. While his wife went through the pain and toil of bringing four children into the world as quickly as she was able, he visited and talked, drank tea, walked and argued, with Miss Firth and her father, and led the social existence which he loved. The Firths were good, not to him alone, but to all his family, including his sprightly sister-in-law Miss Branwell who relieved him of half the worry of his delicate continually pregnant wife. Miss Branwell stayed a full year with the

Brontës at Thornton, and when she returned home to Penzance, to charm the young men again as a superannuated belle and marry none of them, Miss Firth and Mrs. Brontë wept together.

Mr. Brontë brought no cheerful females with him to Haworth to engage his humour at tea time. He liked their society, their flattery and his own gallantry which in the past had more than once taken him out of his depth into love.

He neither comprehended women nor made any pretence of understanding them. His passionate love terrified and fascinated them, his domestic affection when passion had cooled down was not conspicuous. If he had any, he hid it very well, and was outwardly, even in his children's eyes, cold, autocratic and subject to violent disturbances of equanimity.

Mr. Brontë visited Thornton but rarely after he left there, although it was but a few miles distant. After Mr. Firth was dead and Miss Firth gone away and married to the Reverend James Clarke Franks, this double bereavement was too much for him and he resolved not to visit the scene of his past happiness again. He made no new friends at Haworth, found no one congenial to his mind. The friend of his life was Miss Firth, and he honoured and loved her to the end of her days.

At home Mr. Brontë was lonely. He had an immense and somewhat pathetic pride. Was he not the master of a wife and six children? In whom can the king confide? He was perfectly the master of his family in so far as his perceptions permitted him to be. His wife did her duty, but she perversely took ill of a mortal illness directly she got to Haworth. Her uneasy husband retired to his study and, though only forty-three years old, gave way to dyspepsia. So far his life had been a progress; now progress and growth had ceased, disintegration had begun. He did not know how to cope with disintegration. Fear entered his soul, his temper became the worse for it.

Within doors, the good sense he appears to have displayed in public forsook him. He came to wear a vague defeated look about the house, like a dog that does not understand the misfortunes that befall it. His health became in his own opinion very delicate. As a refuge from the perplexities of his life he took refuge in old age, and attained an absolutely venerable appearance before he was fifty-six.

Outside his home Mr. Brontë was respected by his new parishioners, if not liked. He had brains in his head and Yorkshire men tolerate brains of a practical sort. His fine physique, his discretion or lack of interest, his prompt charity, his common sense, and the tenacity with which he held even unpopular opinions if he conceived them to be right, were fully appreciated. Interference is the unforgivable sin, a sin of which Mr. Brontë was not guilty. Strong tales were told of his peccadilloes by his sturdy passionate neighbours with gusto and pride, with relish of the parson's failings: he ill-treated his wife, let off pistols, he bashed his fist through doors, sawed off the backs of chairs, slashed silk gowns, cre-

11

mated hearthrugs, in the paroxysms of his frightful temper. All that happened at the Parsonage was known at the Black Bull, and there Mr. Brontë's actions became invested with the dignity of fable.

He had one added grace. He was a poet, and though oblivion may enshroud poets of another country, Yorkshire is proud of its local bards, especially if they can claim the dignity of print. Poverty of inspiration is no blot upon the genius of our poets; the printed rhyme is practical evidence of poetic worth among us, if so be that it is attended with reason.

When Mr. Brontë at length realized that death would some day deprive him of the exclusive possession of his wife, he sat down in his study and allowed his dyspepsia to get the better of him and put the servants to the trouble of serving his dinner in private that he might have quiet in which to digest it. To become invalid oneself is an extraordinary form of pique, a retort addressed to Fate not seldom indulged in by the selfish when there is genuine illness in the house. In time, bronchitis and blindness reinforced his ill-health, but now disappointment, and perhaps hidden sorrow, sorrow for lost friends, for his wife's decline, a sense of frustration and the death of personal ambition made him restless and easily vexed. He used to work off his suppressed feelings and his resentment in long tramps over the moors, in the pistol practice that gave rise to his reputation as a furious individual, and in occasional outbursts of temper when he imagined that strict

12

obedience was not shown to those commands which he conceived it was his right and duty to give.

Up to this moment his life had been an almost continuous progress, but now the days of progress were over. In his time he had been both brave and stubborn, both ambitious and silly. Everything of which he was possessed he had earned for himself, with the assistance only of his excellent health and clear determination.

His father was an Irish peasant, Brunty or Prunty by name, his mother a Catholic pervert or Protestant convert. Her conversion was one of convenience and no doubt not fundamental. He had nine brothers and sisters.

After a smattering of school he became a weaver, until at the age of sixteen, with about as little education as Oliver Goldsmith, he took to teaching in a Presbyterian school. But egged on by the patronage of a Mr. Tighe he decided to improve his station in life. Thereupon from his assortment of religions he selected that of the Church of England, and presented himself in due course at St. John's College, Cambridge, whence after four years he emerged a clerk in Holy Orders. He had contrived to get rid of the worst part of his brogue there and possibly to improve his manners.

The Reverend Patrick proceeded at once to Wethersfield in Essex as a poor and handsome curate. He at once, too, fell in love. His love letters are said to have been of the most terrifying ardour and to have thrown Mary Burder, the object of his passion, into fits of apprehension. Her relatives took strong exception to him, and, to enforce their opinion, locked Miss Burder up in her bedroom and intercepted his correspondence.

Mr. Brontë showed throughout his life an admirable submission to the ways of Providence; outside of his public career as a priest, he was the merest puppet in the hands of destiny.

Not receiving any answer from the imprisoned Miss Burder to his letters, he left Essex, probably confirmed in his opinion of female inconstancy, and within a year appeared as curate of Dewsbury in Yorkshire where very presently he engaged his unwanted affections to Miss Maria Branwell, a cheerful, pious, thoughtful young Dissenter from Penzance. Miss Maria was her own mistress, and had a fortune of about fifty pounds a year. As he earned a sufficient income himself, with her money they were able to marry directly he obtained a proper house in the neighbourhood.

A few years after their marriage they moved with their two first children, Maria and Elizabeth, to dear Thornton of happiest memory, where four more children, Charlotte, Patrick Branwell, Emily Jane,[1] and Anne, crowded into the world.

Anne was barely christened before the whole family removed again from the pleasant vales and society of Thornton to the bleak isolation of Haworth.

Thus at a stroke, Mr. Brontë lost almost everything

---

[1] Emily Jane Brontë, born July 30th, 1818. Baptized at Thornton Chapel, August 20th, 1818, by the Reverend John Fennell, her maternal great-uncle.

that he had striven to attain, intelligent society, political interests, and a sphere of expansion for his intellect, and was cast out amongst peasants and uncultivated manufacturers again to conclude the last forty years of his life on the edge of civilization, above his original level it is true, but alone above it.

There he dwelt among his neighbours in civility but not in intimacy, afraid of intimacy, of contracting the smallest obligation. His children were born of what he had become, and he walked among his gently bred family with the unease and pride of a self-made gentleman.

II

SIX SMALL CHILDREN

"I've never caused a thought of gloom,
A smile of joy, since I was born."
Emily Jane Brontë

THE Brontës established themselves at Haworth with little ado, for they had no new curtains to hang up, and no carpets to lay.[1] Their old-fashioned Georgian furniture, the chairs with horse-hair seats, glass fronted bookcases and slender four-posters, were soon disposed in the low-ceilinged dove-grey rooms. Matting was laid in the study and parlour, the painted tin cannisters were ranged on the kitchen mantle-shelf, the grandfather clock set to ticking in the hall. Everything was soon polished up to its usual brightness.

The four middle children marshalled by Maria resumed their quiet lives. Anne, the baby, probably lay in whatever arms were free of labour at the moment, or cried in her cradle. Maria, careless and untidy, sang the most beautiful songs and told endless stories to those who could understand them. She was just six years old.

[1] The poverty of the Brontës has been dramatized. In country places in Yorkshire, the purchasing power of money was extraordinary, even at the close of last century. See Appendix I.

The little den over the hall that looked out upon the graveyard was dedicated to their use. As Maria read the newspaper to her charges and taught writing and reading there, it was called the children's study.

When summer came, she trailed such of them as could walk out on the moors, and sometimes they probably remained there all day without proper food, with only crusts of bread and spring water for dinner and endless make-believe to pass the time.

They saw less and less of their mother. She lay in her room unable to contemplate their future without the blackest forebodings.

Toward winter she became very much worse of the cancer that had fastened upon her, and had to have constant attention night and day. A woman was got in to nurse her, but no one, I feel, took particular care of the children, except Maria who reared them as well as she was able. Summer returned, and Mrs. Brontë became yet worse, and as she became worse, very naturally the children were more and more left to themselves.

Their father saw them at breakfast, and not again perhaps all day. They dined alone in the parlour or picnicked on the moors, and spent their evenings in the kitchen with Nancy and Sarah Garrs. At night Maria, Elizabeth, Charlotte and Emily, Patrick and perhaps Anne, now slept in the little den, crowded in somehow. They were not very big, it is true, and people lay closer in those days than they do now. Maria took one or another of them in her arms, little Patrick often, and told tales of far-off days as the rain beat

17

upon the black panes of the uncurtained window. Maria's tales were not always soothing. In the drear stillness of a winter night her vivid imagination would conjure up visions of Calvary, of things awful and divine, which only her presence made bearable. But between the newspapers and the Bible, Maria's knowledge seemed quite inexhaustible, and her wisdom profound. The others loved her as they might have loved their mother who lay dying in the next room, with the instinctive love and admiration that little children have for their mothers, which is something akin to the innocent love of simple people for angels and heavenly things.

In the course of the autumn of 1821 in their second year at Haworth, Mrs. Brontë died. She was buried in the church beyond the garden wall, and the children were put into crêpe.

Rumours spread through Haworth that she had died of ill-treatment and a broken heart, rumours that had no justification, for though Mr. Brontë was severe and stern, he was not cruel.

These rumours came round to the children as such things will, by the servants, no doubt, who forget that children can hear and understand. Charlotte remembered them all her life, but what did Charlotte not remember? The servants early discovered that they had better mind what they said in her hearing.

For another year after their mother's death, Maria continued to act in her place. The six little black-robed creatures trailed after her onto the moors, and there, I think, became not so gentle and meek as they appeared to be in the house. There is little doubt that Branwell and Emily "grew more wild and reckless daily."

If the childhood scenes in *Wuthering Heights* contain any memory of the long past, Emily of the dark curling hair and the big grey eyes led a wild free life. She would not suffer any repression, and was as naughty as a high-spirited child can be.

She was prone throughout her life to answer back, and it is not likely that at the tender age of four, she was more polite than at twenty. A sensitive, ardent, loving little thing she must have been, for very early, perhaps in these days, she suffered a repulse that ruined her happiness forever. She believed firmly in after days when the morbid mood came upon her that she had never been loved, that she was a waif cast into an alien, cruel world, that no one had ever cared whether she lived or died. She imagined at the age of eighteen that she was friendless and alone, and had always been so since the day of her birth—had been the unwanted child.

Though members of a large family, Charlotte and Branwell and Anne, too, harped on the orphan child motif. Charlotte perennially introduced herself into fiction as an entirely orphaned and only child. But Emily added to her orphan's estate the woeful loneliness of a waif—"a waif for twenty years."

Why in her poetry and her prose alike does there appear so often the black-avised and stubborn child,

19

a mournful boy, a creature that pretends to like to be dirty in contradistinction to others? That glories in a savage mien and the freedom of the outcast, and yet dies almost of its longing to get into heaven, a heaven of love?

I feel that there came an hour when "having behaved as badly as possible all day, she sometimes came fondling [to her father] to make it up at night . . ."

"Why canst thou not always be a good lass?" he enquires sadly.

"Why cannot you always be a good man, father?" leaps out in reply.

The awful thing has been said, the mark overshot. The child has destroyed forever the bond of respect between herself and her parent. She waits aghast for the wrath to come. No expected wrath breaks forth to justify the child; instead there comes a sigh.

"Nay, I cannot love thee. Go, say thy prayers, child, and ask God's pardon. I doubt thy mother and I must rue that we ever reared thee!"

Outcast, the poor creature creeps away and weeps frightful tears in the dark, in secret; and on that night the father dies in the child's heart, and it is she who has killed him. Animals and children carry their mortal wounds into dark corners and howl the lament of Hope.

III

MR. BRONTË SOLVES A DOMESTIC PROBLEM

"A cap more awful than a crown."
Shirley. Charlotte Brontë

MEANWHILE Mr. Brontë was casting about for a new mother for his orphaned infants, or female solace for himself. He must have been unutterably lonely. His only companion was Maria, aged eight, with whom he read the newspapers and entered on those political discussions which laid the foundations of his children's attitude toward the world, if not toward life. Probably at this time he began to entertain them with those hair-raising tales that early fomented their imaginations. He seems to have been a splendid raconteur if a namby-pamby poet, and having probably no conception of childish intelligences, luckily for them, did not water down his stories for the ears of his little audience. The Brontë children were reared on strong meat.

Outside of the innocent flattery of his children's attention, Mr. Brontë can have had no joys. Rumours of his treatment of his wife spread and spread; of how he starved his children on potatoes, and what-not to his discredit. Of these rumours I believe he was ignorant, which serves to show his isolation among his rough parishioners.

It is said that in his extremity he applied to Miss Firth of Thornton, whom there is no doubt whatever he dearly loved and honoured, to take upon herself the motherhood of his six children. She was possessed by the death of her father of a moderate estate and fortune, but I do not believe that this circumstance weighed with Mr. Brontë. In April, 1824, she left Thornton, and was about this time sought in marriage by her future husband, the Rev. James Clarke Franks. It was in that year, perhaps, that Mr. Brontë revived a feeling in his mind, if not in his heart, for his old love Mary Burder, and renewed his suit, but Mary Burder thanked her God that she had not married her late lover and refused to be persuaded. He never attempted again to remarry.

During these attempts to secure the blessing of a new wife, he made shift with a foster-mother for his infants, his sister-in-law, Miss Elizabeth Branwell of Penzance, who had lived as part of his family at Thornton. *She* had replied favourably to his suit, and in 1822 arrived at Haworth with all her worldly goods, Japan dressing-case, ivory fan, silver teaspoons, gold snuff box, and eyeglass, to take charge within limits, of one nephew, five nieces and a disappointed man. One can understand why she came to Haworth, but why she stayed is another matter; perhaps she liked the independence of her position, for she had not to honour and obey Mr. Brontë, while yet she was mistress of his house.

Miss Branwell was a small social body, like her niece Charlotte, with set ways and old-fashioned notions. She took snuff and wore great caps with a frill half a span in depth sticking out round her face, and several yards of love-ribbon bunched upon the top. She embellished this headgear with a frizzled forelock which, if "front" as it was called had the same meaning then as in my childhood, came away with her monstrous cap at night.

She began at once to grumble of Haworth, the Parsonage stone floors, the cold. To keep her feet off the stone floors she clicked about the house stilted upon pattens.

Nothing was to her taste at the Parsonage, nor indeed in cold inclement Yorkshire. She retired to the late Mrs. Brontë's bedroom with its bleak view of graves, currant bushes and lean thorn-trees, its trembling echo to the passing bell. There she made the most of a meagre allowance of morning sun. There she kept up a perpetual fire in the grate, and a shocking stuffiness you may be sure, and sat in a stiff chair dreaming of the palms and fuchsias and tea parties of Penzance.

Now, when Aunt Branwell came to the Parsonage, a general freedom must have pervaded the house outside of Mr. Brontë's limited range of vision. She found herself confronted by a slatternly and gentle girl of eight, in the shelter of whose shadow hung five children, Elizabeth, who has left no impression on time; Charlotte with piercing critical eyes and a terrible sense of justice; Branwell the boy, wild, red-haired, insinuating and much caressed Emily Jane, stubborn and strong, and perhaps already hard, as children who conceive of themselves as outcast are hard, and Anne, a small pale baby thing. Only Maria and Elizabeth seem

23

to have remembered the mother. The other four enjoyed Maria's innocent version of maternal love.

Aunt belonged to an age when girls were brought to virtue with the birch rod applied to the palm of the hand, a species of bastinado that sometimes had fatal results. Minor cases of evil doing were treated with thimble raps upon the skull or boxings of the ear. Stubborn sinners were locked into dark closets and entertained to bread and water. Her notions of female propriety are said to have been narrow.

One has to remember the age in which these children lived. One has to remember that Aunt Branwell, though independent in character, was not intellectual nor bound to her nieces by ties of intellect. They inherited from their father a passionate temperament, and lively pleasure in things of the mind. Aunt brought shirt making, carpet sweeping, and the strict attention to p's and q's forward as the end of female endeavour, and preached neatness, submission and duty as the cardinal virtues.

It is out of all likelihood that she studied the individualities of the children she came to tend. Individuality was then a matter for regret. Many must have been the tussles of will between Aunt and Charlotte, and Aunt and Emily. In after-life Charlotte prevailed over her Aunt—not without stiff battle—but, nevertheless, she prevailed.

Miss Branwell was no poor relation. She had her fifty pounds a year, her savings and the right to dispose of her money by will. An Aunt of independent character and independent means is not always an easy personage to have set over one. When those in subjection were generously endowed with imagination and temper, and she in supremacy had no conception of the needs of lively minds, of the scope of childish intelligence, or the depth of childish genius, one would imagine that there must have been grave collisions between ruler and ruled, before the children learned as children do, that the tyrant has not half their own resources, their own power of intellect, and is in fact a mere figurehead of circumstance.

The following chapter is entirely apocryphal, an attempt to get back to the years of Aunt Branwell's reign, when all the children were alive at home together.

The years of early youth, the time of the dawn of consciousness, are the most important of a man's life. I hold that by the age of twelve a human being has experienced both the highest and the lowest emotions of which he is ever to be capable. He has been by that time all that he may perhaps become. If children were capable of full expression of their inward experiences, of their flights of fancy, of their sufferings, of their joy, what works of genius would the world contain! When I think of past rapture and past sorrow, I envy my youth. Yet at the time how titanic I felt my sufferings, and how frail I found my nerves to suffer them! How I prayed to attain the calm, dull age of eighteen! Then I thought I should be fitted to bear amongst other things death of those I loved.

We who write, who create, seek and seek for the pure

25

experience. If we are able to look back to our youth we shall find it. Far from being immature, experience was then most complete. With age, experience becomes lumbered with worldly trash, and dulled and dried. Between us and our youth, alas, lies the quagmire of adolescence, in which our early days are drowned and suffocated. Whether or not we are conscious of it, our mature endeavours are a struggle to revive from that death, an attempt to re-awaken from that sleep and that forgetting.

IV

THE FIT

*"I thought the swift-darting beam was a herald of
some coming vision from another world."*
Jane Eyre. Charlotte Brontë

*"An undefined, an awful dream,—
A dream of what had been before;
A memory, whose blighting beam
Was flitting o'er me evermore."*
Emily Jane Brontë

I HAVE no grounds whatever, but the works of
Charlotte and Emily, and various reactions of
Emily's in after-life, for supposing that what I am
now about to write is true. The original suggestion
came from an eminent psychologist, and seems to me
to be of such value that I have made an attempt to
establish it as fact.

Somebody had a fit. The fit was caused by imprisonment in a room associated with death. A strong imagination conjured up ghosts and phantoms. A light
shone. The victim screamed. "Unconsciousness closed
the scene."

Such is the gist of the narrative in *Jane Eyre* of that
child's fit in the late "Mr. Reed's" bedroom.

Charlotte recounts this episode in her usual precise
and logical manner. The most significant lines in the

27

account are—"I thought the swift darting beam was a herald of some coming vision from another world," and "a sound dulled my ears, which I deemed the rushing of wings." The whole business of this fit is complete and rounded off in Charlotte's story of it. In the middle of the affair "unconsciousness closed the scene." It is important to emphasize that point.

Something happened to Emily in her early days, some episode of imprisonment. Prison is the theme of much of her poetry. In solitary rooms she casts herself upon the floor and weeps. Unconsciousness does not close the scene; it would seem that for her the experience only then begins.

First we have:

> "I imagined in the lonely room
> A thousand forms and fearful gloom."

The victim prays to God that she may die:

> "And then a voice—I hear it yet—
> So full of soul, so deeply sweet:
> I thought that Gabriel's self had come
> To take me to my Father's home."

Jane Eyre says:

"I wiped my tears and hushed my sobs, fearful lest any sign of violent grief might waken a preternatural voice to comfort me."

Emily says:

> "Three times it rose, that seraph-strain,
> Then died away, nor came again;
> But still the words, and still the tone,
> Swell round my heart when all alone."

28

What Jane Eyre fears to hear is the solace of Emily Jane's life. This seraph song—phantom thing—radiant angel—soothes her anguish in all but the very blackest moments for the rest of her days. In her worst times of despair she cries indeed:

"O Dream! where art thou now?"

But it is the dream, the vision, "sometimes dear, though false," the "angel that nightly tracks that waste of frozen snow," her "phantom bliss"—her "messenger of hope," that returns endlessly though she doubt its reality, to refresh her courage in the dungeon that she so often conceived her life to be.[1]

I have often been told by one who understands these things that the seraph-comforter of dreams and poetry is *always* to be traced back to some actual memory of maternal protection—the mother bends over the bed to soothe the child in nightmare—some mother-craving is satisfied suddenly by a protective gesture. There is a fiercer craving where the mother is dead or never known, or dimly known.

I believe that Aunt Branwell, in a misguided attempt to correct Emily, shut the poor child up one winter's afternoon in the room where Mrs. Brontë had died. The light began to fail, and Emily began to think of the Mother she could not remember. I believe she dreaded to imagine the dead returned, angel-dead her Mother

---

[1] How the seraph-comforter changed his aspect as time went on, and became the seraph-demon, time will show.

would be to her. A natural beam from some transient lamp carried through the churchyard pierced the uncurtained windows. Emily shrieked and had a species of fit in the midst of which Maria came to her, and in her half-consciousness Maria's form and tender words seemed the fulfilment of a vision. Maria's voice had the strange cadence of a voice heard through dreams.

In after-life, Charlotte used to become afraid for Emily when she got into those white cold rages which opposition sometimes roused in her. Why was Charlotte afraid if she had not had some experience to warn her?

The more I think upon it, the more I feel convinced that Emily had a trance or fit in a room where she was imprisoned, in the death chamber of her dimly-remembered mother. There alone with her mother's death-bed, it is easy to imagine what she waited for in the wintry dusk. A light flashed into the room, perhaps the light her liberator carried. It was too much: she screamed. The expected thing she dreaded to behold had come. It dissolved into an angel voice, and a beautiful reversal of nightmare took place at the very climax of her terror. Small wonder that a visionary comforter haunts the darkness of her poetry, the dungeon darkness, and often attends those frightful dreams that beset her in later days.

To return to Charlotte's story of the Fit. She had read Emily's poetry before she wrote *Jane Eyre*. She remembered no doubt the circumstances of Emily's imprisonment. Beyond the heralding beam (Emily's "blighting beam") and the rushing of wings (Emily's "strange sensations—Heralds of me"), her account does not proceed.

In Emily's memory the circumstances are vague, the episode of unconsciousness is vivid.

Emily gives her age as barely six when this affair took place.

One last point. Charlotte had a marvellous power of re-creation, little if any power of creation. Her veracity was remarkable, her invention weak. The more one reads her books, the more one suspects that everything in them echoes to a fact. She covered her tracks by the flimsiest changes of names, of age, of locality. Truth as she saw it was her muse. Certain of her acquaintances thought that she worshipped Truth with considerable indiscretion.

V

THE MASK

"I knew the wish that waked that wail;
I knew the source whence sprung those tears:
You longed for fate to raise the veil
That darkened over coming years."

                              Emily Jane Brontë

" 'And I hadn't an idea of it. To think of me never
even suspecting it. Strange! Strange!' And then he
talked about Emily and the other sister, and told me
how he had considered Emily the genius of the fam-
ily, how he never fancied Charlotte capable of writ-
ing anything."

                    The aged Mr. Brontë in conversation with
                              Mr. John Stores Smith

ABOUT this time Mr. Brontë tried a curious and pathetic experiment upon his children in order to discover if possible what went on in their little minds. He thought he saw precocious signs of talent amongst them. For nine years of his life Mr. Brontë had been a schoolmaster, and furthermore in the course of his present duties came into contact with other children frequently. He was therefore accustomed to a supervision of the mental processes of the young, in so far as these processes touched the acquirements of knowledge. Already he used to regard his

32

eldest daughter Maria as an intelligent companion, to whom he did not need to condescend.

Thinking that perhaps his children knew more than even he gave them credit for, and that they were perhaps shy of answering his questions in the open, he conceived the idea "that if they were put under a sort of cover [he] might gain [his] end." There speaks old Brontë, Charlotte's father—gain his end! There happened to be a mask in the house, one of Miss Branwell's accoutrements of vanity, perhaps—the time was not long past when women wore masks on many occasions. He made his children put on that mask in turn and answer his questions boldly from behind it. The questions were dry, the answers highly moral. Only Emily's showed any vigour:

"What shall I do with your brother Branwell?" asked the father.

"Reason with him, and when he won't listen to reason, whip him."

Emily was nearly six.

So much for Mr. Brontë's experiment. Though he could mask and unmask his children's faces, he could not unmask their hearts. Did he know that Charlotte "began to analyze character when she was five years old," and certainly now in her eighth year had got a proficiency in that business? Did he know that in a silent hour the portals of futurity opened before Emily? That a grim vision of the coming years cut her "off from hope in early day?" Emily has but to recall early childhood to break out into mournful thoughts: " 'Tis

33

true she stands among the crowd, an unmarked and an unloved child;"—"Never has his grim fate smiled since he was born."

If Emily attempts to describe happy children, or indeed happy people, she creates something pale, insipid or simply stupid, as if she could not comprehend such creatures, or quite believe in them. The gloom of Emily's child-memories is frightful. She can sometimes just recollect a bright, innocent infancy, but her awakening to consciousness was a rude one.

Had her father any conception then or afterwards of the black visions she brooded over? I think she early began to wear that mask of reserve and silence which covered her soul till Charlotte wrenched it off in 1846. Until Charlotte found Emily's poems in 1846, and cut and altered and edited them, I think no one was supposed by Emily to suspect her secret life behind that silence and reserve and harsh aspect which she showed to the world.

We do not know how much Charlotte knew of Emily's childhood. Shirley, who is said to be Emily, is not introduced to us until she is twenty-one. One feels that like Emily's poems, Shirley is Emily edited by Charlotte and cut down.

How much did Mr. Brontë see of Emily's real character, or rather perceive of it, during those long years she spent cooped up at Haworth? "[He] told me how he had considered Emily the genius of the family." Various members of the Brontë family have been voted to that office. The world elected Charlotte, his in-

34

timates Branwell, Mr. Brontë and Mr. Héger, Emily. Did the lonely father see himself in her and feel that she was the only other male spirit in his house? It seems likely. She early knew the boy in herself and later knew the man. Others knew it too.

There must have been an awkwardness and deep silence between Emily and her father, and a hate from Emily towards him that covered unknown to him and herself a sympathy. They were a couple that but for Charlotte and the stiff conventions of the age might later on have gone as far downhill on their respective roads as the flighty Branwell, and they might then have known each other.

Emily's portrait of her father in old Mr. Earnshaw of *Wuthering Heights* is an extraordinary and touching reparation, one feels, for those few lines in her poetry written in a bitter mood:

"Frown, my haughty sire! chide, my angry dame!
Set your slaves to spy; threaten me with shame:"

and:

"My master's voice is low, his aspect bland and kind,
But hard as hardest flint the soul that lurks behind;—"

Her portrait is perfectly fair. It contains no flattery, and those who wish to feel how the child Emily and her father got along together had better read most carefully the first chapters of *Wuthering Heights*.

I am again being rash, writing what I know and cannot prove, but I can see the ageing parson, looking ridiculously like the frog-footman in *Alice in Wonderland*, sitting in that bare, almost elegant parlour at Haworth, choked up in the absurd dignity of his immense muslin neckcloth. I can see him sitting by the fire drumming his fingers on the arms of his chair and cogitating the enigma of the exasperating Emily, whose love seems uncommonly like rudeness to him, whose craving for love is beyond the comprehension of a man who takes for granted love between father and child, and who takes for granted Original Sin and his own supreme authority. She gives him nothing but the hardest feelings, because his code is not her code. They have broken with one another recently, and he has seen her tortured recently. They do not make anything of one another, save that he feels an uncommon bond beneath the formulæ that he has accepted instead of paternal sympathy, save that she feels he is a hard, just judge, just according to the code she knows, unjust according to the code she feels. She imagines she is "now forever cast out of his favour and mourns not for her sudden fall."

She wears now, and for twenty years, the mask of perfect indifference before her father. She fears long neglect might break her spirit, and to prevent that, shows in defence, a hardness in which she thoroughly believes.

VI

COWAN BRIDGE

" 'Tis dangerous to provoke a God
Whose power and vengeance none can tell;
One stroke of His almighty rod
Can send young sinners quick to hell."
The Rev. Carus Wilson in *The Children's Friend.*

"Little girl, here is a book entitled the Child's
Guide; *read it with prayer, especially that part con-*
taining 'an account of the awfully sudden death of
Martha G———, a naughty child addicted to false-
hood and deceit.' "
The Rev. Mr. Brocklehurst in *Jane Eyre.*
Charlotte Brontë

IT was decided by Mr. Brontë almost immediately after the affair of the Mask to send his two elder daughters, Maria and Elizabeth, to school; Maria was now ten, and beyond reading, writing and very little arithmetic was practically ignorant. She did not even sew well. A woman in those days who could not sew was indeed in a savage state. In spite of no skill with her needle and a feeble knowledge of geography, Maria has left a tradition of brilliance and precocity beyond that even of the other children. Elizabeth stopped short at reading and writing.

At various distances from Haworth lived certain

37

friends and connections of Aunt Branwell and Mr.
Brontë who probably were concerned in this decision
to send the girls to school: Uncle Fennell, Miss Branwell's uncle; the William Morgans, her own cousins;
the Franks and the Outhewaites. Though these
families are lost sight of by many biographers, I believe
that they had considerable to do with the fates of the
Brontë children. The Morgans lived at Bradford, the
Fennells at Crosstone, the Franks chiefly at Huddersfield. The men of these families were in the Church.
Miss Outhewaite was Anne's godmother and a great
friend of Mrs. Franks. Aunt Branwell used to stay with
her Uncle Fennell,[1] taking sundry of the children with
her from time to time.

All these parsons no doubt heard with appreciation
of a project put into execution about this time by a
wealthy brother of the cloth, the Reverend William
Carus Wilson of Kirkby Lonsdale, for providing education for the daughters of poor clergy at a very low
cost.

To this school Mr. Brontë decided to send his daughters. In vindication of him, it must be stated that the
school had not yet proved itself good or bad, that it
had been but just got together.

It was situated not far from Kirkby Lonsdale at a
spot called Cowan Bridge, in an old mill house and row
of cottages adapted for the purpose. The fees, about
£15 a year, paid in advance in half yearly instalments,

---

[1] Uncle Fennell was the first art-patron of the Brontë children. He flattered them by keeping certain of their childish efforts.

were within the power of all but the poorest curates. The name of the institution was The Clergy Daughter's School.

I am not going to repeat all that Charlotte Brontë has to say of "Lowood" in *Jane Eyre,* with which school Cowan Bridge has been identified, nor rake up the seventy-five-year-old controversy as to whether or not it was a hell for little children.

Those who are curious to know what a charitable institution for girls may be like need only visit one of those barracks called orphanages which rescue the infant destitute to-day.

They will be received in a pleasant house, sometimes ivy-covered, sometimes quaint and old, where the authorities, three or four overworked teachers, congregate; where the head mistress lives and the parson calls. Behind this human region is a gaunt edifice, brick without, and painted brick within. Concrete stairs, bare boards (scrubbed by the children), high, glaring windows, howling draughts, odours of carbolic, cabbage-water and hot fat, make up the ground floor. Above stairs, bare high dormitories, narrow flock beds, odour of sour boots and stale garments, and the same howling gale invite the little prisoners to repose.

The food is as grim as the building. There is usually some arrangement made by which it is to the benefit of the housekeeper if the household accounts are kept low; in some cases, she profits in inverse ratio to the orphans. Even in institutions where charity does not hold sway, burnt porridge, joints charred outside and raw at the centre, soggy potatoes, and cabbage like boiled brown paper are the rule. What then where charity pares down the cost and pays the cook?

As for clothes, the usual uniform of these abodes of love is contracted for per age and not per size, it seems. The stiff, strong boots fit nobody, the stuff frocks are made to nobody's measure, the hats suit no one, the hideous cloaks hang heavy on the neck. Cleanliness is next to godliness, but nobody is really clean.

I know the charity look and the charity smell.

Nowadays no kindly epidemic comes to relieve the stark lives of the poor little wretches in these horrid spots. Modern charity is germ proof, but in Mr. Brontë's time "low fever" and "decline" were prepared to remove all weakly children and did the office competently.

Over Cowan Bridge in supreme authority presided the Reverend Carus Wilson, who administered the funds paid in by parents and such extra money as the public chose to give.

He was a great authority on Damnation and Sudden Death, Humility and Usefulness. His intentions were excellent, but his God was frightful. He seems to have faithfully served his ogre of a deity.

To this man's scheme of education and redemption, Maria and Elizabeth were submitted on July 1st, 1824. Charlotte joined them on August 10th; Emily, who read very prettily and sewed a little, on November 25th.

They were each taken to school by their father, who

inspected the place and dined with the children at the common board. Mrs. Franks called at the school in the autumn and gave the children half-a-crown apiece.

I do not know what stock their father and his friend took of their health on these visits. Some of the children had but recently had measles and whooping cough, so that doubtless the continued cough of Maria and Elizabeth was put down to the latter lingering complaint.

However, on February 14th, 1825, Maria was fetched home on advice received from the school by Mr. Brontë and died in May of "decline." On May 31st he had to fetch Elizabeth. Charlotte and Emily were removed the next day. Perhaps he had at last awakened to the danger his children were in. Elizabeth died in a fortnight also of decline.

Meanwhile, "low fever" (dysentery, typhoid or typhus) attacked the school, but it was not because of this that Mr. Brontë removed his children. That probably was too familiar a pest at Haworth to agitate him. Extraordinary as it may seem, none of the Brontës took that disease.

A scandal followed the epidemic, and the school was removed from Cowan Bridge and re-established at Casterton on improved lines.

How did Emily, who seems to have found home tyranny unendurable, enjoy these days at school? "The younger children in all larger institutions are liable to be oppressed," wrote A. H., a teacher at Cowan Bridge in Brontë's time; but the exposure to this evil at Cowan

41

Bridge was not more than in other schools, but, as I believe, far less." [2]

Children have had their nerves ruined for life by exposure to the tyranny of girls and boys of ten years older. Betwixt her seniors and the sword of damnation which hung ever ready to strike the errant scholar out of life one cannot imagine that Emily found the love and hope that were the craving of her existence.

We know nothing of her sufferings at this place, but we know that several years later when she went to school again "her health was quickly broken: her white face, attenuated form, and failing strength threatened rapid decline—" and that after the age of twenty at school in Brussels, "the same suffering and conflict ensued." Moreover between these two experiences as a scholar, she underwent a period as teacher herself, which time was marked by nightmare and poems of nightmare. The very idea of school was repulsive to her. If all I feel is true, through misunderstanding and through accident, she had learned the nature of Hell at home. Cowan Bridge very probably completed that lesson.

In after-life, Emily certainly had a prison complex as I believe it is called. Rules and regulations, anything that suggested prison, threw her into a frightful state—prison, prison—it is all through her poetry—dungeons, thrall.

[2] From the *Journal of Education*, January, 1900. See *The Brontës*, Clement Shorter, volume 1, pages 69 and 70.

"Oh! dreadful is the check—intense the agony—
When the ear begins to hear, and the eye begins to see;
When the pulse begins to throb, the brain to think again;
The soul to feel the flesh, and the flesh to feel the chain."

43

VII

THE DEATH OF MARIA

". . . we, at rest together,
Used to lie listening to the showers
Of wild December weather;
Which, when, as oft, they woke in her
The chords of inward thought,
Would fill with pictures that wild air,
From far-off memories brought;—"
From *Caroline*, by P. B. Brontë

"I hold another creed, which no one ever taught
me, and which I seldom mention;—" "it makes Eter-
nity a rest—a mighty home, not a terror and an
abyss"—"with this creed revenge never worries my
heart, degradation never too deeply disgusts me, injus-
tice never crushes me too low: I live in calm, looking
to the end."
"Helen Burns" in *Jane Eyre*. Charlotte Brontë

"I—the image of light and gladness—
Saw and pitied that mournful boy."
From *The Two Children*.
Emily Jane Brontë

THAT Maria Branwell was the original of Helen
Burns in *Jane Eyre* there can be no doubt. I
have quoted Helen Burns' creed from that
book at the head of this chapter, and for a very definite
purpose. It was not Charlotte's creed. Never for a

44

minute did Charlotte live calm. But though it was not Emily's creed either, it was a belief she fought to hold. Helen Burns thought that Man was "perhaps to pass through gradations of glory, from the pale human soul to brighten to the seraph." The seraph of Emily's darkness is perhaps here, "the image of light and gladness," which visited her many and many a time in later life.

I think that Emily's poems, *The Two Children* and *Child of Delight, with Sun-Bright Hair*, are written of herself, the mournful boy, and Maria, the seraph whose "erring wing" wafted her "down to weep with him."

Death, angel, comfort, were three associated ideas in Emily's mind, fixed as a triumvirate over her imagination, by that episode of the fit. Maria who comforted her in consciousness, who held this bright comforting creed, died. Maria the comforter became dead, became an angel.

Here is a catastrophe that takes on itself the memory of that other catastrophe. The imprisonment of Cowan Bridge has obliterated, or rather taken on the memory of, that first imprisonment, and in the long years to come the first imprisonment plays havoc with Emily's soul in dreams and rises to vision-power in her daydreams; the second imprisonment, complete with comforter and death, alone remains consciously remembered.

I have quoted what is said to be part of Branwell's recollection of Maria, though it is but a ghost of recollection. He remembered her as a teller of objective tales. Her sisters remembered her as one who spoke

45

subjectively of spiritual things, from whom they received impressions of other-world glory. Branwell, in his poem *Caroline*, appears as a girl child—Emily in *The Two Children* and *Child of Delight* as a boy. Apart from illustrating the tendency to interchange of sex in poetry this has a further significance. Because I feel that these poems are extraordinarily important in Emily's history, I will quote them fully, although they are long. They are memory poems, two of The Lonely Child Poems, and come, I feel, in memory, chronologically after that one beginning "Come hither, child; who gifted thee," which is the Fit poem.

Here appears, very early in her life, that creature who is destined to become in time the unregenerate, pagan, superstitious, Heathcliff.

The Two Children

Heavy hangs the raindrop
  From the burdened spray;
Heavy broods the damp mist
  On uplands far away.

Heavy looms the dull sky,
  Heavy rolls the sea;
And heavy throbs the young heart
  Beneath that lonely tree.

Never has a blue streak
  Cleft the clouds since morn;
Never has his grim fate
  Smiled since he was born.

46

Frowning on the infant
  Shadowing childhood's joy,
Guardian-angel knows not
  That melancholy boy.

Day is passing swiftly
  Its sad and sombre prime;
Boyhood sad is merging
  In sadder manhood's time:

All the flowers are praying
  For sun, before they close,
And he prays too—unconscious—
  That sunless human rose.

Blossom—that the west-wind
  Has never wooed to blow,—
Scentless are thy petals,
  Thy dew is cold as snow!

Soul—where kindred kindness
  No early promise woke,—
Barren is thy beauty
  As weed upon a rock.

Wither—soul and blossom!
  You both were vainly given:
Earth reserves no blessing
  For the unblest of heaven!

Child of Delight, With Sun-Bright Hair

Child of delight, with sun-bright hair,
  And sea-blue, sea-deep eyes!
Spirit of bliss! what brings thee here,
  Beneath these sullen skies?

47

Thou shouldst live in eternal spring,
    Where endless day is never dim;
Why, Seraph, has thine erring wing
    Wafted thee down to weep with him?

"Ah! not from heaven am I descended,
    Nor do I come to mingle tears;
But sweet *is* day, though with shadows blended;
    And, though clouded, sweet are youthful years.

"I—the image of light and gladness—
    Saw and pitied that mournful boy,
And I vowed—if need were—to share his sadness,
    And give to him my sunny joy.

"Heavy and dark the night is closing;
    Heavy and dark may its biding be:
Better for all from grief reposing,
    And better for all who watch like me—

"Watch in love by a fevered pillow,
    Cooling the fever with pity's balm;
Safe as the petrel on tossing billow,
    Safe in mine own soul's golden calm!

"Guardian-angel he lacks no longer;
    Evil fortune he need not fear:
Fate is strong, but love is stronger;
    And *my* love is truer than angel-care."

Compare this boy in his morbid strength, with the colourless "Harriet" in *Caroline*, and when it comes to deciding whether Emily really wrote *Wuthering Heights* or Branwell did, remember the comparison.

48

VIII

HEATHCLIFF IS BORN

"That iron man was born like me,
And he was once an ardent boy:—
Emily Jane Brontë

" 'Who knows but your father was Emperor of
China, and your mother an Indian queen?—' "
Nellie Dean in *Wuthering Heights.*
Emily Jane Brontë

WHETHER I am right or wrong about the exact incidents of Emily's infancy, I am right in the nature of them.

She was a child of the most ardent, loving, generous and jealous nature, and episodes that would perhaps have left unmarked a stolid vegetable child wrought upon her disastrously.

Impetuous spirits of her kind ask and need quick, and perhaps violent, response to their emotions. They are easily deeply wounded, easily feel shame, and what is worse, imagine neglect, to them the most intolerable thing on earth.

Neglect, real or imaginary, makes these wild ardent spirits hard, black, morose, at least in their own fancy; and since they must enjoy heightened emotion of one kind or another, when love does not supply their needs to the full, they fall back upon self-pity, and see them-

49

selves as exiles of the most, I want to say, colossal loneliness. Enormous pride glorying in enormous loneliness, Satanic pride in the loneliness of Satan reigns in their bosoms. We get such thoughts as

"I am the only being whose doom
    No tongue would ask, no eye would mourn;

and

"Weaned from life and flown away
    In the morning of thy day."

People no doubt will say that infants cannot realize loneliness nor grasp the meaning of Hell. True, I was nine or thereabouts when the black revelation was made to me, when my soul itself was terrified. But the Brontës were precocious children.

There descends upon some men and women out of a mysterious region beyond what we know as rational, a dark spirit, which possesses itself of the most unlikely souls, and houses there to depart unbidden as it came. Sometimes this creature takes itself off on holiday, leaving its host in bewilderment and despair, sometimes it would seem to survive as "ghost," the mortal body in which it dwelt. Those in whom it condescends to take up its abode leave the pleasant ways of life and cleave to its dark ways. This creature I have called the Dark Hero, the man of All or None. Whether he attaches himself to a mediocre and vain family in Corsica, to a close-fisted narrow bourgeois French family, to one of a stubborn conventional Irish parson's brats, whether he selects as host a courtly lyric poet, or a man who tried to be a perfectly ordinary New Yorker, it makes no difference: the creature of his selection becomes more him than themselves, becomes him, with his sense of exile, his craving for domination, his continuous melodrama of self-pity, his longing for escape. But over and above this he possesses a perfect certainty of his own damnation, and sees love which is identical with heaven in his mind, as the unattainable, the not-for-him. This spirit, this seraph, this redemption, this not-for-him, I call the Fair Lover.

The Man of Destiny, The Season in Hell, Heathcliff, Paradise Lost, Captain Ahab,—the Dark Hero takes a number of names and bemoans his exploits under many titles. Barely disguised in some borrowed character, he walks abroad and awakens in the human breast a dangerous sympathy. He rushes away from the common world into exile, and while bemoaning his exile, exalts his escape, cries at the same time "I am free" and "I am damned," and has nothing but the pride of his own loneliness to congratulate himself upon, like a recusant priest who has forsaken the world for God, and God for himself, and finds himself the symbol of the devil.

D. H. Lawrence says of Melville, who escaped to sea from Puritan America, who ran away from his home (to look for what? The perfect lover? The great white whale? Christ?)—Lawrence says of Melville who lived in a whirl of torture—"he was born for purgatory." Well, yes, if purgatory is that spot where the self-outcast bemoan freedom, and the would-be-damned long for

Paradise. On the whole the Dark Hero makes no bones about his hell. Milton did an excellent piece of work when he drew the devil's portrait, Rimbaud made a masterpiece of Hades. Another of the tribe cried out:

"No promised heaven, these wild desires
Could all, or half fulfil;
No threatened hell, with quenchless fires,
Subdue this quenchless will!"

That may be, but nevertheless the quenchless will seeks with passion of a kind conceived by few for an unpromised heaven, and the word "threatened" before "hell" is mere rhetoric for the sake of balance. Hell is not threatened, it is known, just as you or I know our own house, it is splendidly known.

Lawrence says for instance:

"If the Great White Whale [Moby Dick] sank the ship [*The Pequod*] of the Great White Soul in 1851, what's been happening ever since? Post-mortem effects, presumably."

If he does not mean Utter Damnation by that I do not know what he means, and yet—why went Lawrence to Mexico? "Childe Roland to the Dark Tower came," and you or I want to know what he sought there. Lawrence goes to Mexico, and Rimbaud to Abyssinia, and Melville to the South Seas, and Milton to Paradise Lost, Napoleon to Destiny, Emily Brontë to the paleolithic moors, to find out.

To return to Emily Jane, aged seven, at home in a grim little village perched on the edge of our world.

Emily was the merest child with the same inconstancy as most children, the same readiness to be beguiled out of the sulks by pleasure, the same desire to be spoiled and treated, and set up above her two sisters and her brother as a paragon of perfection, not moral perfection, but as a paragon of cleverness, wit, and beauty.

The paragon of cleverness and wit and beauty in the Brontë family was almost certainly Branwell. Charlotte had her position as head of the family, a position that suited her taste. Charlotte was as plain as a pikestaff and knew it. She had a feminine love of ordering the ways of those about her. It is interesting to see how early she got a grip on the family, and how finally she possessed herself of the whole of it. Charlotte carved herself a way through life, but for Branwell, swift impressionable creature, swift, too, in his small limbs, the Future was reserved.

That was the age of boys, of eldest sons at any rate. These young gentlemen were designated "my son and heir," though they might be heirs to nothing; "young Hopeful, the Hope of the Family," as if parents, brothers and sisters clung to this son in a permanent state of family despair; indeed, in many families, the eldest son was hailed as a small Messiah of sorts. While mothers and sisters bowed in adoration, they loaded the poor wretch with many of a Messiah's responsibilities. They made his shirts, worked his slippers, and if poor, ate bread and cheese that he might eat meat, the while they fainted in his arms, and clung to his coat-tails as he fought his way through life. They became his slaves,

53

but made him their Providence. Little tiny Branwell with his freakish mop of red hair, had the prospect of acting Providence to three sisters. That, of course, was not stated in full and definite terms; that was the little surprise Fate reserved to spring upon the hero many years later if she thought fit. She never had the chance to spring it upon Branwell. In the meantime he was simply the hero with the reins of Juggernaut Future placed in his hands by his family, which car was painted in brilliant and fascinating colours.

There is no doubt that Emily craved his place, and that she was jealous of him and envious, and resentful of her female situation. Emily never did things by halves; nor as a matter of fact did Charlotte or Branwell. It was not in their nature.

Had she held Branwell's place, who knows what might have happened? But she did not, and accordingly threw herself out and exiled herself, and solaced her jealousy with contemplation of the unrelieved blackness of her future, in rivalry to the unrelieved brilliance of his. In this mood she welcomed, without perceiving what precisely she welcomed, "a dirty, ragged, black-haired child" of no name and no country with whom she speedily fell in love, who became fictitiously *the first favourite of her father,* got the better of her elder brother, and soon got the better of herself. He became duly "more myself than I am." He came from nowhere, did this Lascar, "fit for a prince in disguise." Who knew but his father was Emperor of China and his mother an Indian Queen?

Thus very early in her day, in secret, in imagination, she began to foster and love a dark soul in herself, a dark thing that grew and grew upon her and ultimately possessed her, body and soul.

It is not accident that Heathcliff was first favourite with Mr. Earnshaw, nor the rival of Hindley Earnshaw; it is very far from accident that Heathcliff began early to hate Hindley and to nurse revenge and finally ruined him. What name Emily gave herself in those early days when she was Heathcliff I do not know, probably none. Nor do I know precisely when she welcomed in her dark counterpart. These beginnings are vague.

He seems to have come before Maria's death, judging from the two poems quoted in the last chapter. There is every indication that she began to lead the double life of herself and Heathcliff very, very early.

Whether she realized this double life, what proportion the dark half of it assumed in regard to her whole life is impossible to tell; how intermittent or if intermittent at all—these things must remain secret. In her black moods it is represented as perfectly continuous and all-obliterating. As time went on, other people began to notice, not that she had two lives exactly, but that she was more like a boy than a girl. M. Héger, of Brussels, her schoolmaster there, discovered that she had a male mind. The thing was in full possession then.

Thus did the Dark Hero come to one of its victims— in infancy—taking advantage of jealousy, disappointment, rebuff, to establish a firm footing. It blackly glorified loneliness, prison, oppression, and set its host seeking in hell for that spirit about whose feet "three rivers ran," set him seeking "in heaven, hell, earth, and air, an endless search, and always wrong," for the Spirit with the "dazzling gaze," for the fair Lover, Christ, the Great White Whale.

Once indeed Emily craved wealth and riches, those promises that hung in the air about Branwell. Those toys were the first bright thing she longed for—and to be fair-haired and fair-skinned—everything, in fact, that she had not and was not. Princes and Kings and all the dream paraphernalia of childish ambition carried her thoughts away to a land of make-believe where she became of course splendid, all powerful, but if I read aright, still dark, avenging and exiled.

In our ignorance of human life many incongruous things appear in such a life as hers, or Melville's or Rimbaud's. We don't perceive as yet, what I ought to call the ground plan of such histories. What seems irrational and topsy-turvy is most certainly not. Why did Melville prefer apparently the dirt and labour of a whaling ship to the Paradise of the South Seas; or Rimbaud throw up poetry and turn private in an army; or Emily burden herself with the dirty work of her home? Why did Rimbaud take up with the weak Verlaine, and Emily with the weak Anne? Why did they not all, like Napoleon, make for domination? They were irresistible. The Dark Hero can prevail against everything but Heaven.

I have suggested many questions which probably I

cannot answer, and having lighted these fires I will leave them now to burn, and come back into the world and look at Emily the child in an ordinary light. Remember, however, as we watch the ordinary Emily at play with her brother and sisters, that Heathcliff is born in her, that within she is a boy beginning to seek the Fair Lover, the White Spirit, under cover of a darkness in which she knows hell. Her secret life is occupied with many things which do not appear to concern her, and with many longings, but first in fury among her many desires is a wild desire for the secret of Paradise and to make the Holy Spirit subservient to her will.

There will come a moment when as I say she becomes fully possessed by this Dark Thing. Then in prose and poetry she will expose him to the world in a singular, complete and unique fashion, knowing not, of course, the full significance of her exposition.

IX

EMILY AND CHARLOTTE

"I have at last my nameless bliss
As I love—loved am I!"
Song from *Jane Eyre*.
Charlotte Brontë

"Thee, ever-present phantom thing—
My slave, my comrade, and my king."
Emily Jane Brontë

IF Emily had by now a secret hero in her own bosom
—"always, always in my mind: not as a pleasure,
any more than I am always a pleasure to myself, but
as my own being"—Charlotte, head of the family since
Maria and Elizabeth were dead, had also her private
desire. If Emily was what she was to become, Charlotte
also was complete of her future self.

Charlotte is the most curious compound of passion
and orthodoxy, of genius and duty that ever was welded
together by an iron determination. She, too, had her
hero whom she sought, and alas for her, found but
could not get. But he was a material being, a protector,
something she could submit her dominating will to, with
whom she could exhaust her tremendous fund of human passion, with whom she could renew it.

Charlotte, too, had lost a mother twice, as it were.

This curious girl, finding no real protector to hand

in the days of her youth, manufactured an ideal protector out of reality. She betook herself very soon after the death of Maria to the bosom of an ideal parent —a father—to the dream bosom of a Duke of all things, the Duke of Wellington. Since, too, she must have friends, a craving which she did afterwards properly satisfy, she made a magnificent corps of friends out of the allies and associates of this august adopted parent.

Here we get the similarity and the difference between Emily and Charlotte.

They both sought love. Love was the craving of their lives, but Charlotte's ideal love was within material limits and looked for from a material source, whereas Emily's lover was looked for in realms beyond the narrow boundaries of common human life.

Beside her craving for a real and definite love, Charlotte had a very concrete passion for her own way, for arranging the lives of those about her, for general administration. To be first was not much her desire. She had her father's stubborn character. When Charlotte made up her mind to anything, she got it in the end. She was the stuff from which Florence Nightingales are made. Duty and necessity were the mainstays of her soul, actually of her soul. On two occasions in later life, if not more, she would have shipwrecked as Branwell did, but for duty and necessity. They all had it in them to sail on to the rocks in a blind tempest except, maybe, Anne.

Charlotte's vices were inability to yield an inch, and a horrid partiality for tampering with the lives of others. Both are female vices. She thought meanwhile that she was a creature of submission, capable of absolute submission to the object of her love. When women talk a deal about submission I doubt but they are of the domineering sort, of the eating-up sort, husband-ogresses. There is too great a disparity between their self-abasement and the god-like husband of their dreams for truth. Such lowliness and such heavenly height can never mate. The wives that creep in the fiction of their imaginations about their husband's feet get hold of a Twelve Tables of the Law made out of stone with which they rise and club their poor god on the head if he dares to step down off the pedestal which they have arranged for him.

The Twelve Tables of the Law, in the hands of such as Charlotte, are indeed of a Roman strictness and patrician rigidity.

It was with such a character that Emily had to live. Charlotte, soon after they settled down at home on their return from Cowan Bridge, quietly took the lead among the Brontë children and kept it. But for her a number of things that happened later would never have come to pass. But for her I should not now have to recall Emily from oblivion as the Witch of Endor recalled Saul, to produce but a possible semblance of reality a dream, that may either terrify the beholder or make him cry "Faugh! 'Tis nothing but a ghost!"

Well, Emily and Charlotte settled down at Haworth, if to settle down is an expression compatible with their existences. Charlotte was nine, Emily rising seven. As far as we can tell, Charlotte set up a friendship with Branwell that lasted until he sunk so far below her that she could not do with his presence, when he became so loathsome in her eyes that she threw him off. Emily was therefore reduced to Anne for a companion. Anne had been spared the nightmare of Cowan Bridge. She was a little thing, rather like Branwell in feature. She had violet-blue eyes and a lovely skin, whereas Emily was pasty with dark curls. Aunt petted Anne, melancholy doll of a thing who cherished, she tells of herself, from early childhood the doctrine of Universal Salvation. Which of the children did not nurse some unchildish doctrine in her bosom?

These four children, Charlotte and Branwell, Emily and Anne, whether settled or not, began to lead at last a regular life, though Branwell's regular habits perhaps were already not above reproach.

The girls, however, were good enough and their days monotonously alike to outward view.

They rose betimes at six or seven and took a breakfast of porridge with their father in his study. Miss Branwell only quitted her chamber when she had exhausted the possibilities of the morning sun. At breakfast old Mr. Brontë seems to have been at his best. He told the children tales of the past doings of people who had lived near and about Haworth, terrible tales to curdle the blood. I say he told these tales at breakfast because that is the tradition, but it may have been after tea in a gloaming and infinitely more uncomfortable hour.

"They were full of grim humour and interest to Mr. Brontë and his children, as revealing the characteristics of a class in the human race, and as such Emily Brontë has stereotyped them in her *Wuthering Heights*," said one who had heard the old man telling of them.

There are plenty of somewhat ghastly stories extant in Yorkshire, the victims of which would not thank me for repeating in order to bear out the style of thing Mr. Brontë recited.

After breakfast if the newspapers had come—*The Leeds Intelligencer* (Tory), *Leeds Mercury* (Whig), *John Bull* ("high Tory, very violent"), or *Blackwood's Magazine* ("the most able periodical there is"), according to Charlotte, aged nine—Mr. Brontë read and discussed the news with his children. It was 1825, Byron was but recently dead on an heroic adventure in defence of Liberty, his dust was thoroughly winnowed by the Press. Reform and the Catholic Question violently agitated public opinion. Sir Walter Scott's affairs toppled over between this year and the next. The Duke of Wellington, who had saved England from the Scourge of Europe, was making enemies in politics.

After the hour with their father the girls took lessons of sorts with their aunt. As far as I can gather she taught them nothing but domestic matters, deportment (old style) and patience. They remained ignorant in all branches of elementary learning except Scripture, General Knowledge and Literature. Emily in particular never learned to spell. "Neither Emily nor Anne was learned," says Charlotte after their death, "they had no thought of filling their pitchers at the well-spring of other minds." Charlotte spent every minute of her life that she could spare filling her pitcher thereat. Aunt taught her nieces sewing—shirts, bands, under-linen, their own ugly old-fashioned clothes; she taught them housework, sweeping and so forth. Emily became in time an excellent general servant.

"Emily is in the parlour sweeping the carpet."

"Emily is upstairs ironing."

"Emily does the baking and attends to the kitchen."

Emily gets up and does all the roughest part of the household work before the rest are astir.

That is about all her sisters have to tell of Emily during her lifetime.

I own that almost all other reference to Emily has been lost or burnt or cut out or suppressed.

After a morning devoted to various tasks the children dined at midday in the parlour with their Aunt. The food was monotonous: plain joints, vegetables and milk pudding. Charlotte did not touch meat. This is the only confirmation I can find of the story that Mr. Brontë brought up his girls exclusively on potatoes, bread and milk. Charlotte had eaten no meat for several years when she went to her second school, and there she had to conquer a strong distaste for it. Mr. Brontë continued to dine alone.

The afternoon one imagines was devoted to sewing and rambles on the moor until tea; tea, with talk, more newspapers, lively intelligent arguments between old

Brontë and Aunt Branwell, concerning points in the books they read together.

The children often spent the evenings with their favourite servant, Tabby Brown, in the kitchen. Tabby had come to the Parsonage while they were at Cowan Bridge. She was elderly, old-fashioned and entirely Yorkshire. She spoke pure dialect, used outlandish words and broadened every vowel in the alphabet, so that people from another county understood not a single word she spoke. In this tongue she sang the children ballads and told them tales of the "fairish" (fairies) which lived in the Bottom before machinery drove them away, stories of "the graves under the rectory back kitchen," of witches running red-hot needles into human flesh. Joseph's dialect in *Wuthering Heights* was hers. She stood no nonsense from the children, but she loved them, and they loved her, I think, more than either their father or aunt. Wondrous indeed are characters of Tabby's kind. They are rough. Superficially their intellects are back to front. Time, space and distance are vague notions to them, but they know the fundamental principles of life and bide by them and defend them to the death. Such people are never servants in the common sense, but part of the family with duties strongly conceived, rights tenaciously held, and a ready jealousy. They are familiar with the family soul, and more faithful and honourable in the keeping of it than many a member of the family itself. It is impossible not to have rows with people of this sort, but the rows are usually begun by the brave folk themselves,

64

and touch some matter of slighted authority or injured honour. As a rule they end happily with the benign forgiveness of the offended one. The worst rows arise, however, from suggested benefits some member of the family would confer. Then the doubtful mind begins to "suspicion on" the honesty of the would-be benefactor. Privileges out of order are not welcomed. They destroy the independence and make obligatory sundry acts which the will would otherwise perform unasked.

The Brontë family had often to go very carefully with Tabby Brown, especially in matters of interest to herself.

Tabby's ballad-singing and story-telling had to be over by seven, when the children were summoned to bed; Branwell apparently retired to his father's room, where he shared the night with old Brontë and his pistols; the girls, one gathers, still slept in the den over the hall, three of them instead of five, it is true, and continued to sleep there till Aunt died.

The day was done. No great change took place in the order of it for several years, but there developed in the quiet lackadaisical procession of hours those far-famed pastimes of the Brontës that were to end in the novels of Charlotte and Emily and Anne.

There developed also in the secret hours that underlay these quiet moments Heathcliff and Lucy Snowe, despair and—I hesitate to call it—renunciation. I do not think Lucy Snowe understood Heathcliff. I doubt they ever really met. They clashed and struggled, being thrown by fate incongruously into the same family.

Lucy admired Heathcliff in the end, in the bitter end, but meanwhile—Charlotte tried to bring up Emily in the way she should go. Mind you, I admire Charlotte tremendously, one has to admire such constancy, such bull-dog fortitude and tenacity, but what a tragedy that she should have got her teeth into Emily and, I cannot help feeling, as the years went on torn pieces unwittingly out of her soul.

X

CHILDISH PASTIMES

"I am the Duke of Wellington."
Charlotte Brontë

*"Yes—I could swear that the glorious wind
Has swept the world aside."*
Emily Jane Brontë

CHILDREN who live in lonely country places have long hours on their hands with nothing to do, nothing immediate to think about, no one but themselves to talk to. It was that way in our house. We occupied our leisure in mischief and pretending. When I was six or thereabouts and my sister five, I became the aunt, and my sister the mother, of four imaginary, intelligent and talking cats. These cats are still "alive, well and active." At night as we lay in bed in the dark we suddenly grew up and were transported to Amsterdam which we had never seen, an Amsterdam of quaint old houses and canals. The cats had for a father a fictitious man, Sir Edward Compton, Admiral of the Dutch Fleet. He wore a short pointed beard and was a drunken and dissipated character. He used to pay surprise visits to his wife and feline family and startle them by peering in at a window at night with a drunken leer on his face. Ultimately he went to Australia and perished miserably of drink. I can see Sir Edward's dissipated face peering in at a certain dream-passage window to this day.

Those were golden times. I had contracted a love affair at the age of three with a boy of seven. Romance occupied several hours of the day. This young man ultimately became in my mind uncle by marriage of the Compton cats, grew up at night and was also created an Admiral of the Dutch Navy. On his flagship the cats sailed round the world visiting many strange lands. He was clean-shaven.[1]

Long before I was nine I became aware of beauty. The pink buds of a sycamore tree against a blue and white March sky. The sycamore tree grew above our ash-pit. The ash-pit was roofed with an ivy-tod. Behind it was a crenellated wall, very old, with an old door in it and round steps up to the door. My first picture. A burnt sienna wall and a Prussian blue sky. Divine! Prussian blue and burnt sienna! Blue sky, pink buds! Ah! Oh, dear! A pain like love at my heart. The pain I felt for the cats' future uncle.

Thus do children begin to awake in the world.

Beyond the sycamore was the high-walled kitchen garden; beyond the garden a valley; arising about the valley the moors. In October, the first snow whitened the moors. Then I forgot cats and love and longed to be up there in the vast white silence, to see the white hares playing in the old shale pit, the black ice on the

[1] A curious parallel between our game and the Brontës'. Each of these cats possessed an island. The isolation of islands seems to appeal to the young mind, to satisfy childish craving for dominion.

68

moor pools, to hear the eternal chorus of the grouse, "Go back! Go back!"

In winter the moors are other-worldly. The low northern sun sets at three in the afternoon in long slanting rays. Twilight is green and cold and silent. Night closes in before four o'clock, closes in like death, in narrowing circles of gloom, with threat of cruel cold or snow. It is well to be off the moor by then, well to flee from the ghosts of lost travellers, for every year travellers are lost on the moor; from goblins, from ancient terrors of the Roman Road, monstrous Druid shapes.

It is grand, strange, frightening to be born and bred in a house against the moor, to dwell in an outpost of this world on the threshold of another, to live in the roaring of the equinox and full blast of the blizzard. How the wind thunders in autumn and tears and screams in March! Some folk hear ghostly bells tolling in the wild deep wind, unearthly music sounding, unearthly cries.

The wind pours down over the moor like a sea broken loose. It shakes and batters the house as it thunders down into the valley. It screams at the eaves, howls in the chimney, suffocates man and beast, the fire on the hearth, the grass on the heath.

Children and animals within doors become excited and a little mad. The children hope the worst will happen, the roof blow off,[1] the end of the world come.

[1] I believe a chimney stack did actually fall down one wild night at the Parsonage. There is a reference to such an event in *Wuthering Heights*. It was recalled probably to Emily's mind by the collapse of the tower in *The Entail*. See E. T. W. Hoffmann's *Weird Tales*.

Glorious terror! It is impossible to exaggerate the terror and the glory sensitive children feel amid the strife of elemental forces. It is of the nature of genius.

Children love terror. When there is none in the elements they manufacture it. Children adore the Absolutely Awful, the Extraordinarily Wicked, provided there is a tolerable chance that it will all come right in the end.

"It is well known that the Genii have declared that unless they perform certain arduous duties every year, of a mysterious nature, all the worlds in the firmament will be burnt up——."

Little Charlotte Brontë's letter to the Editor of a Magazine of which she was Proprietor, Printer and "dear reader" epitomizes that terror which honest children would confess to be divine. Unless! Unless! Unless I get indoors before I can count ten and am standing on the parlour sofa, devils will get me body and soul.— I must be across that wall, I must, I must, before the first star comes out, or the sea will arise out of the east, the Great Wave will overwhelm me!—Which of us has not propitiated a ghastly Fate by some such arduous duty? I never dared to fail, and never did fail, in the antics I performed to stave off the End of the World, the Great Wave, the very Devil.

But children love, too, the Perfectly Good and Noble.

Charlotte Brontë worshipped "the great duke in green sash and waistcoat" whose words were like precious gold, "the august father" of Lord Charles Wellesley and the Marquis of Douro. This man dominated her existence in childhood, she was in love with both his sons, though Lord Charles perhaps had precedence in her heart. She put them all to live on an island, fifty miles in circumference, Vision Island by name. She built the Iron Duke a palace on the banks of the River Lusiva. She enslaved her brother and sisters to him. Branwell, Emily and Anne offered homage to this demi-god, this Titan. Disguised as Sir Walter Scott, John Bull, Michael Sadler, a hundred others, they rallied round the Tory standard as other children have rallied round the standard of King Charles or Bonnie Prince Charlie.

"I am the Duke of Wellington!" cried Charlotte at the age of nine. She identified herself with her hero in those games they used to play. She was also the Marquis of Douro and Lord Charles, lived every moment of their imaginary lives and wrote in their names lengthy tales and autobiographia.

"Our plays were established; *Young Men*, June, 1826; *Our Fellows*, July, 1827; *Islanders*, December, 1827. These are our three great plays, that are not kept secret," writes Charlotte in 1829. The Duke figured in *Young Men*, possibly also in *Our Fellows*, which was founded on Æsop's Fables, but the *Islanders* was the Duke's play par excellence.

"The play of the *Islanders* was formed in December, 1827, in the following manner." According to Charlotte writing in 1829, "One night, about the time when the cold sleet and stormy fogs of November are succeeded by the snow-storms, and high piercing night

71

winds of confirmed winter, we were all sitting round the warm blazing kitchen fire, having just concluded a quarrel with Tabby concerning the propriety of lighting a candle, from which she came off victorious, no candle having been produced. A long pause succeeded, which was at last broken by Branwell saying, in a lazy manner, 'I don't know what to do.' This was echoed by Emily and Anne.

"*Tabby*. 'Wha ya may go t'bed.'

"*Branwell*. 'I'd rather do anything than that.'

"*Charlotte*. 'Why are you so glum to-night, Tabby? Oh! suppose we had each an island of our own.'

"*Branwell*. 'If we had I would choose the Island of Man.'

"*Charlotte*. 'And I would choose the Isle of Wight.'

"*Emily*. 'The Isle of Arran for me.'

"*Anne*. 'And mine should certainly be Guernsey.'

"We then chose who should be chief men in our islands. Branwell chose John Bull, Astley Cooper, and Leigh Hunt; Emily, Walter Scott, Mr. Lockhart, Johnny Lockhart; Anne, Michael Sadler, Lord Bentinck, Sir Henry Halford. I chose the Duke of Wellington and two sons, Christopher North and Co., and Mr. Abernethy. Here our conversation was interrupted by the, to us, dismal sound of the clock striking seven, and we were summoned off to bed."

Next day all these Islands began to amalgamate into Vision Island, which became in time a huge agglomerate of fact and fiction, enchantment and geometry.

Beside these public games, Charlotte had secret or

Best plays with Emily "established," some on December 1, 1827, the others in March, 1828. These plays never developed a literature as the others did, vast masses of manuscript written in a handwriting to scale with mice.

But over and above all games of imagination, over household tasks and the daily round, frowned the moors. Behind the Parsonage were two or three fields. The children had but to cross the fields and they were in "a little and a lone green lane," a rough sandy ditch of a lane, the banks covered with fine moor grass, with patches of bilberry and heather, with the harebells in their season. In spring these moorland roads become rivers, in winter they are often filled level with snow between the loose stone walls above the banks. Though all the children delighted to escape by field and lane into the wild region of heather and wind, it was Emily who loved the moors. Love is a tame word for the rapture she felt up there under Heaven. There she became a bright aërial creature who laughed and sang and ran wild. There she was gay among the others and led with Branwell over moss and stream. But the others never knew, not even Charlotte, the ethereal gaiety that Emily was, when incarnate child became disincarnate as the shining music of Heaven merely because she felt the moor-wind that blows clean through heart and body, and blows both away.

XI

EMILY AND THE MOORS

"What have those lonely mountains worth revealing?
More glory and more grief than I can tell:
The earth that wakes one human heart to feeling
Can centre both the worlds of Heaven and Hell."
                                        Emily Jane Brontë

"—it is only higher up, deep in amongst the ridges
of the moors, that Imagination can find rest for the
sole of her foot: and even if she finds it there she
must be a solitude-loving raven—no gentle dove."
                                        Charlotte Brontë on Emily Jane

IF I were to quote all that Emily has sung and said
of the moors, and to comment thereon in the light
of my own feelings, this book would lengthen to
distraction of the reader—for here would be an escape
from the world and all that is in it, and a panegyric of
wind and weather, full of hyperbole and other madness.

For the most part our moors are as bare as the back
of your hand. Charlotte said that those who seek beauty
there "must bring it inborn: these moors are too stern
to yield any product so delicate." That may be the
opinion of many. I will not attempt to disclaim "the
drear prospect of a Yorkshire moor." But, even at the

mere recollection of those bleak brown uplands, there is a mounting madness in my mind, as I once said many years ago.

The moors are primeval; perhaps that *is* why they repulse many folk and are meaningless to others. The old primeval passions wake there still, with the old monotony and timelessness that cares nothing for an hour or a million years. The moors care nothing for you or me, as you or me, nothing at all. They know neither time nor man.

A child of innocence is at home there. The old primeval moods cause the innocent heart to race and innocent feet to rush in a wild career, innocent arms to fling out in a wind-embrace, and eyes of innocence to shine upon blue flower, delicate frost pattern, or dizzy weavings of a waterfall.

By innocence, I do not mean that sweet quiet associated with Heaven, but an ancient state of soul that existed before men asked is there a God? If man knew God he felt Him in himself, and if he knew the devil, was the devil.

Up there, on a bright June day or a sparkling winter morning, to Emily and to me—

> "A thousand thousand gleaming fires
>   Seemed kindling in the air;
> A thousand thousand silvery lyres
>   Resounded far and near."

The moors sing. Air and heath in summer, the taut keen frost in winter. We think it is the music of the empyrean, therefore it is so for us.

Have ever you heard the world go round?
Up there wonder and worship and fear come clean
to the heart and overwhelm the reason.

> "—lovelier than cornfields all waving
>   In emerald and scarlet, and gold,
> Are the slopes where the north-wind is raving,
>   And the glens where I wandered of old."

In what sense lovelier? In spring the little flowers
hide there beneath the black heather and the black
crags. Only in late August do the moors burn with
purple heather flower, to the careful eye, all shades of
pink and heliotrope and crimson, at sunset red as fire.

> "There is a spell in purple heath
>   Too wildly sadly dear.

Perhaps when we broke loose on the moor we suffered
an enchantment. Visions rose up there more real than
reality, fires kindled in the soul that burnt the light of
common day to ashes.

The moors are not all fulfilment, they are craving
also. Ecstasy of experience and ecstasy of desire.
Though we hear the music of the spheres, we burn with
a heathenish desire for reciprocation. There is hate,
black as night up there.

> "So stood I, in Heaven's glorious sun,
>   And in the glare of Hell;
> My spirit drank a mingled tone,
> Of seraph's song, and demon's moan;
> What my soul bore, my soul alone
>   Within itself may tell!"

76

There is an unrest and black craving in those moors; the unrest of the lost who have seen Heaven and know hell. A backward going from the day of cities to the time when God walked upon the earth in the cool of the evening, for the time before that when the Spirit breathed upon the face of the waters, when the light was divided from the darkness.

Creatures of the moor are not exempt from the strife of the moor. They get a pride, a self-pride that longs for Paradise and rejects Heaven, or perhaps they recognize the moor as home, because the devil's pride has got them by the heart.

No human man or woman could bear the passion of creatures such as these, unless their souls were made of the same strife. Not even then. It is a damnation to succumb to the love of lost souls of the moor.

"I am weary to escape into that glorious world, and to be always there—and to take you with me, you more myself than I am, you Heathcliff, the genius of the moor," says Catherine to Heathcliff.

These two lost souls cry damnation upon each other and betrayal, because the one forsook the other for human love and human purpose.

Now before such as Catherine Earnshaw can live tolerably with decent people, the spell of purple heath must be broken, the moor wind shaken from the hair, the moor light faded from the eyes.

No sane man could stand Catherine for a wife, no sane woman Heathcliff for a husband.

77

These creatures are the dark part in us, the unmatable, the utterly lone.

They have their sweet moments, their moments of beauty and rapture, but their ravings are not comfortable and not good. They do not wish those they love greater torment than they have themselves. They only wish never to be parted from their loves—either in torment or in joy.

"Oh! could that heart give back, give back again to thine,
One tenth part of the pain that clouds my dark decline!"

.   .   .   .

"Oh could I know thy soul with equal grief was torn."

This is the equality that these strange forces crave in those they love.

I said such could not live with decent people. Decent seems a dull little word, but it is the right one. I mean decent in God's sight, which these others are not. Dante had the decency I mean, and so had Saint Francis. Saint Francis went alone to moor places, but there he took his decent love into the light of the sun, and so saw God.

But the dark people go on to the moor to rejoice in the pride of their loneliness, to exalt their exile and their sufferings.

78

XII

GROWING POTATOES IN A CELLAR

"The old church tower and garden wall
Are black with autumn rain,
And dreary winds foreboding call
The darkness down again."
              Emily Jane Brontë

"I told her sometimes they were like growing
potatoes in a cellar. She said, sadly, "Yes! I know
we are!"
     Mary Taylor in recollection of Charlotte Brontë

TO sober down Emily there was, however, a long dull drag of days and hours at the Parsonage. Days when the rain poured in dismal torrents, and sickly fog stirred up out of the valley, days when the snow made the moors impassable, and a bitter east wind caused the blackened thorn trees in the Parsonage garden to shiver in miserable cold. Winter was very long. First endless rain, then fog, then snow and grey winds, then fog and sleet and rain again.

There were few books at the Parsonage until Charlotte later remedied this matter by borrowing from friends and hiring from Keighley lending library. There was nothing but the resources of their own minds to relieve the long dull winters for the four children.

Old Brontë's library does not seem to have been extensive. I imagine it contained *Gulliver's Travels*, perhaps *Robinson Crusoe*. There must have been some theological works. There was evidently some Greek and Latin, Horace for instance, no use to the children except Branwell, part of whose education it was to construe the Odes. "Its collection of light literature was chiefly contained on a shelf which had belonged to her Aunt Mary" [substitute—"their mother Maria"]: "some venerable Lady's Magazines, that had once performed a sea-voyage with their owner, and undergone a storm, and whose pages were stained with salt water; some mad Methodist Magazines, full of miracles and apparitions, or preternatural warnings, ominous dreams, and frenzied fanaticism: the equally mad Letters of Mrs. Elizabeth Rowe from the Dead to the Living; a few old English Classics:—"[1]

There is Charlotte's catalogue of her father's library, detailed in *Shirley*. The mad Methodist Magazines were destined to appear in public later on with considerable success.[2]

Charlotte relieved the tedium with literary composition. The list of her juvenile works is tremendous. Most of them are written in the names of the Duke of Wellington's sons. Amongst numerous tales, poems, histories and what-not appeared four numbers of *The Young Men's Magazines*, and *Blackwood's Young Men's Magazine* "edited by the Genius C.B. Printed by Captain Tree, and sold by Captain Cory," 1829. These and

[1] From somewhere Charlotte obtained the novels of Richardson. Perhaps "Pamela" and "Clarissa" were among these classics.
[2] As Joseph's literature, in *Wuthering Heights*.

the *Tales of the Islanders* (four volumes), 1829-30, were certainly public to Branwell, Emily and Anne, if not partly their creation. They comprise the literature of those make-believe existences begun in 1827, or at least part thereof.

Whether Emily wrote in these early days I do not know. Probably. The Brontës were born writing.

Although so much time was given up to cultivation of the Muse, Charlotte at any rate early began to keep the serious side of life in view. Perhaps in these days before she went to Roe Head School in 1831, Charlotte had dreams of wealth, honour and fame. However, being in the one part extremely sensible, though in the main emotional, impatient and romantic, she early saw that a poor parson's daughter would have to set out some time to fit herself for life, to earn her daily bread. This and a real desire for culture made her, it seems, even in childhood, avail herself of every means of acquiring proper knowledge. She loved acquiring knowledge. That must be stated. She hated household work. It bored her. When Charlotte was bored she was fairly useless, when Charlotte loved she loved for ever, provided she never found her idol false.

Whether literary effort, or learning, or carpet sweeping made the long winters in the Parsonage tolerable to Emily I do not know, nor whether she was bored, chained up indoors day after day with her three little companions: plain, peaked little Charlotte with her piercing eyes, and big-nosed freakish Branwell, and the doll Anne. When people came to the house, Branwell displayed himself cheerfully. He was never shy and stupid. How stupid were Charlotte and Emily? Very stupid, I believe, were these awkward and unprepossessing little objects in ugliest of clothes. Charlotte was extremely self-conscious to the point of physical pain in public—always. Emily, we are told, was uncouth. That she had her dreams of riches and achievement we know. When such as Emily fancy their ambitions are out of range of possibility, they turn resentful and express their resentment in silence and stiffness towards perfectly innocent contemporaries, begin to feel Cinderella and act Cinderella, and cultivate a presence and deportment rigid with wounded pride, a kind of "damn-you-behold-the-neglected-orphan" attitude. "I like it, thank you; I would not touch you happy people with a barge pole."

On the quiet, of course, these stiff-necked folk see no reason why they should not be Joan of Arc or Cæsar, they win wars single-handed, and get given dukedoms whether they be girls or boys; save the King or Queen in their odd moments from Gunpowder plots; and in minor moods rescue the whole family from flaming houses, or make a million or two out of which they dispense enormous sums to their relations, with good-for-evil generosity. The Cinderella business has its compensations.

The combination of slaving in the house and those Gondal legends which Emily began to indulge in later, full of persons of the highest rank on earth, make one suspect that Emily knew the sweets and bitternesses of self-imposed inferiority.

True, in those days girls were definitely inferior to boys, and female self-suppression was cracked up as a virtue, but I cannot help feeling that Emily made herself a martyr to it and defended her independence with unnecessary caution from those above her. Her defences, of course, had their weak spots. Charlotte seems to have known what those weak spots were and to have taken advantage of them for Emily's "own good" or the family good. Alas, if a man cannot see good for himself with his own heart, others had best not meddle. As the old Yorkshire proverb goes:

"Who mell's wi' what another does
Had best go home and shoe his goose."

One thing the Brontës had to be thankful for. Though they were taught that girls should sit on a high straight chair, say "Yes, marm" and "No, sir," and never put their feet on the fender, their minds were not coddled. Between Tabby's ballads, which are sure to have come straight from the natural sources, and Mr. Brontë's tales of local life and Irish life, which if the teller is squeamish cannot be told with any of their natural vigour, the children grew up without any prudery of mind at least. Both Mr. Brontë and Tabitha really belonged to the previous century, and having neither of them cultivated society manners are not likely to have understood that "inexpressibles" was now the right word for breeches nor that "interesting condition"

83

signified a decent natural fact. In their day, which was over, men talked before women in a way that is not done now. Swears and oaths were, it is true, not "*de rigueur*, but up yonder *de rigueur* was not known of, nor anything resembling it in the freedom of family life. I do not know that the children beyond Branwell ever swore. Very probably. Emily and Anne swear very well in their novels. But oaths and plain-speaking apart, there was no censorship of their literature, either in one direction or another, as far as I can see. Murder, vice, natural facts must have been presented to them straight, nay, even ghosts, devils and damnation came out straight upon them from one side or another.

Old-fashioned, elaborate their early style of thinking certainly appears to us, but behind it there was a directness that children reared on circumlocution and the nonsense of stork theories of the origin of man do not show.

Though the children might be feeble in body and small of frame, their minds were well able to endure and assimilate food that many a modern parent would keep from her infant, either because the poor child might learn what it should not, or take fright at night, or not be able to understand. As for not understanding, what does that matter? A child will understand what it can. Better to strain at a camel than to eat a small unnourishing diet of nothing above a few gnats.

Well, the dreary winters, and the summers—in contrast of exotic loveliness—passed slowly on—1825, 1826, 1827, 1828, 1829, 1830. Death kept out of the way and stayed his hand; no catastrophe, good or bad, interrupted life at the Parsonage. One gets a feeling that death and disaster haunted that narrow stone house. It is not so. For almost twenty-five years, apart from removing Aunt in natural course, Death did not visit there. Troubles came of usual sort, but not disaster for many years. Nor do troubles seem to have broken the monotony of the years 1825 to 1831.

The clock ticked in the hall, Charlotte wrote and wrote, Emily learned skill in the domestic arts, Branwell established himself as cock-of-the-walk among the boys of Haworth or wrote like Charlotte, Mr. Brontë grew venerable in his study, Aunt repeated boring tales of Her Past in her bedroom, Tabby conjured up fairies and sang powerful ballads in the kitchen. Rain and snow alternated with the seasons, dreams and reality alternated in the children's minds, Heaven and hell in Emily's heart. The wind rushed down from the moors over all, singing a gay song, howling a dirge. Were not the wind and Emily "friends from childhood"?

Down roared the wind over all; though Charlotte called herself Wellington, and Aunt recollected aloud her conquests of Penzance, and Branwell has been made a present of the golden Future, it is Emily who heard the wind and was roused, and old Tabby who teaches her the measure of her dream, and old Brontë who remembered what it was to work with the hands and labour for his brothers.

Emily belonged to that half of the family, to Patrick

85

Brontë senior and the servant Tabby. They two at heart were of the soil that knows the wind.

I cannot help siding with old Brontë and Tabby and Emily who knew the wind and heard it blow.

XIII

ON THE CONSCIOUS AND THE UNCONSCIOUS

"To-day, I will not seek the shadowy region:
Its unsustaining vastness waxes drear;—"
Emily Jane Brontë

"Speak, God of visions, plead for me,
And tell why I have chosen thee!"
Emily Jane Brontë

THE years go by. It is 1831. Christmas is past. Emily has been stitching at those chemises and night-gowns of Charlotte's which must be got ready for her to take to school, for Charlotte is to go to school again in a few days' time. I do not know whether she wanted to go to school again, or was ordered there, or how it came about. It is of no interest here what the cause was; the point is that she went, and being occupied in affairs of this world, ceased for eighteen months, as far as I can tell, to produce and circulate the works of the Genius C.B., Lord Charles Wellesley and the Marquis of Douro, authors of the dream-world of her leisure moments.

The game was up for the time being as far as Charlotte was concerned.

What of Emily? We have none of her youthful prose

works. It is impossible to say how far she shared in the romance that grew up about the Marquis of Douro and his family, before Charlotte went to school again. Was she Captain Tree or Captain Cory, publisher and book-seller to C.B. and the noble Lords? Charlotte was the only one of the children who ever employed these names. What were those plays in which she and Charlotte privately engaged, which according to Charlotte were never written down? This I feel sure of. As Emily later kept the secret of her Gondal poetry even from Anne, her soul in other words, she did the same by Charlotte in her earlier days. I suspect she did not play fair with Charlotte any more than she did with Anne later on, but kept the significant part of her games to herself. It is very unlikely, considering the later development of Charlotte's character and trend of her genius, that she did not continuously realize the rela-tionship between these games of hers and life. They must have remained for her romances. It is certain that whatever she played, Emily's games were *not* romances, that at this time she led a double life and was in so far conscious of her duplicity that she cheated, as it were, twice; firstly in concealing the fact that *her* playing was real, secondly in playing only superficially when she was with the others. Hence why later did she keep back her Gondal poetry when she was playing Gondal games with Anne, and why was she so put about when Charlotte discovered her poetry?

In my own mind, I have established that, though to all appearances Emily shared games with the others, in fact she did nothing of the kind. I still speak of the early period before 1831 and up to that date. Of course a certain amount of drifting must have taken place. Ideas were certainly begotten in Emily by the others, and her intensity must sometimes have fired Charlotte or Branwell, for ardent natures cannot keep their intensity hid, no matter how they try, not for six years cooped up as the Brontës were. But this I will say: Emily acquired over her inner life an extraordinary control. This control becomes the "I" of the poems, and Nellie Dean of *Wuthering Heights*, the consciousness of self that is so remarkable in her later life. It is different from Charlotte's self-consciousness, this consciousness of self that Emily had.

One does not get dismal visions of the future in infancy for nothing. These previsions make one at the same time both more mature and more childish than one's neighbours. With a revelation or two in early life to go upon, daydreams mean a good deal more than they do to others, and reality is both more intense and dimmer, more intense in anticipation, dimmer met face to face. By reality I mean the common or garden stock-in-trade events of life. A few expositions of the possibilities of experience in early years knock the bottom out of this kind of human life.

Emily very probably would have got laughed at had the others known what these plays meant to her, or thought she would. While Charlotte was airing herself as the Marquis of Douro or what not, Emily was *being* some darkling hero. And she knew it. She knew she was being him. I do not think at this date that she knew she *was* he, not often at any rate. Complete identification comes at first in brief queer snatches, in half moments of vision. Flash! I am myself in my pride, dark, lonely, marvellous, the thing is gone before the thought is quite complete, and leaves one staring at a vision not perfectly clear to the mind's eye, leaves one dreamy and vague. The bed-making or sweeping in hand at the time gets done with somewhat trembling limbs, and there is a craving in the pit of the stomach to get off alone and dream things over or to rush out on a hilltop and run wildly about.

When solitude is achieved the sensation develops into a romance, that clings like St. Elmo's fire about the rigging of a thought. *"He stood there king before all the people"*—something of that kind. Ten, twenty, fifty times the thought burns with romantic light, and nothing comes of it at the moment. It burns and burns in that inner world which the eyes see, wide-open eyes, as blind to the high noon of this world as if darkness reigned. "King Before All the People." There he stands, *I* of course stand, exalted. I have sensations unknown to real kings, probably, but I feel them in the depth of me with my whole being, I know what it is to be a king there "Before All the People." Not my people! I am their king, but they are not my people. Fire blazes out again and again, till sated with exaltation, I return to the world, still dazed and dreamy.

The others are not told about these things. We carry on with them a dangerous game, however, on the fringe, as it were, of our world and theirs. Sometimes we go dangerously near self-betrayal in moments of high spirits. The happier and merrier we are, the more daring we become, but the others who do not go over the border, and are themselves merry and enthusiastic, notice nothing. In triumph we realize that they cannot go over our border at any rate.

I would emphasize here that in melancholy moods the Emilys of life are ten times more conscious than in merry moods. Joy welds them into one being careless and unheeding. In joy they cease to think, have no use for romancing, but are content merely to be. Did ill-health or melancholy never attack them, it is more than likely they would never write poetry or prose, or create the slightest thing of any value. Existence at its height, sheer physical existence, is in itself a most intense delight, far more marvellous than anything they can create. Then they absolutely forget to want to express themselves in verse or whatever they favour as a means of making heaven on earth; and it would be tautology, rhetoric of the most meaningless kind, to set down on paper, paper if you please, in words, what may be felt in unison with the lark in the sky.

In these joyful moments the beauty of the hidden soul shines out, all the beauty hidden away inside the dull ordinary body, beauty such as you and I do not have. It is real and visible. Other people see it in a look or smile and remember it all their lives, particularly strangers.

These moments are not frequent. They often happen in solitude. As the years pass Emily becomes partly conscious *of* them though not *in* them, and keeps them under control: but she never sees what beauty she reveals even though she keeps herself as still as a toad under a rock. Of that she will remain unconscious to the bitter end. And to the bitter end she will never write a line while the gay mood is upon her, but afterwards in the dark times she will write much.

Between joy and melancholy lies a dreary waste, a limbo of discontent and greyness intolerable. Over this reigns other people's commonsense. There is no unconsciousness here nor heightened consciousness. Then one feels less than the dust and is aware of the wheels of time and the grinding millstones of daily life, and they grind exceeding small. There is not poetry in this mood nor any virtue, and it is best to get down to hard work, or else one will go and cry in some corner, drizzly tears like autumn rain.

The dreary waste has its counterpart, of course, a quiet region of content and affection, a homely everyday pleasure in the things that be, in work well done, the bright canisters on the kitchen overmantel, the smell of baking bread. Of all seasons and all times, of all the four seasons of the mind, this is the most beloved. To it belongs the lazy buzzing of bees in summer, the reddening fire of a frosty winter's evening, pleasant gossip and chit-chat, and even high talk without high emotions. This Nellie Dean of seasons is our notion of real happiness.

92

"I'll walk, but not in old heroic traces,
And not in paths of high morality—"

Alas, once we set a-thinking, Nellie Dean flies away like a witch on a broomstick and we are out on the moors in mind, and asking fatal questions—

"What have those lonely mountains worth revealing?
More glory and more grief than I can tell:
The earth that wakes *one* human heart to feeling
Can centre both the worlds of Heaven and Hell."

This is a muddle of a chapter, but so is life as I see it, a fine muddle of the conscious and the unconscious.

One may analyze the part these two things play, but never can a division be made between them, for they are concurrent and consecutive at the same time, in fact, as an old Yorkshire man once said of another matter, they run "simultaneous, one after the other."

I am no scientist, and cannot get down to rock bottom of this realizing and not-realizing business. I can only attempt to present a picture of how some folk can see and not see at the same time. I will try to show how in the course of Emily's life she becomes clear-sighted, not perfectly, but in an extraordinary degree. Alas! as she becomes more conscious, she loses that which she sees. What Emily really wanted was to know what she blindly enjoyed, to see the bliss she only used to feel. See it she did, when she could not feel it. Thus we are back again at what I spoke of before, the wish to command heaven. What an endless circle! She has what

93

she does not see, sees what she cannot have, and the Dark Hero omnipresent in her becomes enraged. At any rate she knows and sees *Him,* at first in flashes as king over the people which are not his people, later on as the complete exile he really is.

XIV

ROE HEAD

"The silver medal, which was the badge for fulfilment of duties, she won the right to in her first half-year."

From Ellen Nussey's account of
Charlotte Brontë at Roe Head.

" 'They took me for a child, and treated me just like one. . . . One tall lady would *nurse me.' "*
Ibid. (Charlotte, aged 15, speaks of a contemporary visit to the Franks.)

CHARLOTTE'S underwear was finished, real underwear, with tucks and buttons and tapes and starch; her drab green dress and collarettes were made, and she set off one winter's day to her new school, leaving Emily more or less alone with Anne. What vanity or lack of vanity made the sisters wear the ugliest dresses in the world, and torture their hair with curl papers every night into a frizz of spirals, it would be interesting to know. Branwell had a frizz by nature. Perhaps it was sisterly admiration.

At any rate, frizzed they all were at this time, and had a passion for great collars and enormous sleeves, Emily in particular. Papa's cravat and Aunt's cap emerged among them in new guise, I think.

Dressed up exceedingly out of date and oddly, Charlotte parted from her family and went forth in search of elementary knowledge to Roe Head near Kirklees, between Leeds and Huddersfield, to school with the Misses Wooler, two ladies who had the art not only of instruction but of happiness. There were not above ten boarders at Roe Head, and these girls, young ladies rather, lived together in a bow-windowed country house more like sisters than schoolmates. The ducal Charlotte, a tiny and wretched little woman with an Irish accent, appeared amongst them shy, awkward, conscious of her oddness and ignorance, but by the summer she had got over the worst part of her ignorance and had made those enduring friendships with Ellen Nussey and Mary Taylor which were to support her in after days.

Charlotte had never been away from home before alone. She was terribly homesick. Every week she wrote to Branwell. She kept on talking to Ellen Nussey about her family, the dead Maria in particular. Ellen Nussey tried to comfort her, even on her first day at school. Miss Nussey comforted Miss Brontë in the bow-window of the schoolroom, and confessed also to homesickness. Miss Brontë cried. The formal address was not dropped, however, between these young women of fourteen for several weeks.

Charlotte was to be ambassador from This World to Haworth. It is therefore exceedingly important to see what this ambassador's outlook on life was, and how she began to conceive those plans in her heart which were to drive Emily almost to distraction.

Ellen Nussey has left a long reminiscence of her at school.

How ignorant she was in elementary school knowledge, how far above her associates in general learning, how she could not play in the garden at ball like the other girls, simply could not—but set the hair on end with her terrible stories of somnambulism, in the dormitory, till she shrieked herself—all this Ellen Nussey recalls to mind, with much more in the same line. It is from Mary Taylor, also in reminiscence, that we get a clearer idea of her mind—Mary Taylor who told her how ugly she was, that her family were like growing potatoes in a cellar, and no doubt several other home truths.

She repeats how ignorant Charlotte seemed in an ordinary sense, how learned in things out of the common range. When her set lessons were concluded she spent her time picking up "every scrap of information concerning painting, sculpture, poetry, music, etc., as if it were gold"—continued to adorn her mind, though she did not adorn her person—and this passion for mental expansion, self-improvement and cultivation of her tastes never flagged throughout the coming years. According to Miss Taylor, Charlotte had in those days "no plan of life beyond what circumstances made for her. She knew that she must provide for herself, and chose her trade; at least chose to begin it once." I suppose—prepare herself to be a governess.

She was terribly short-sighted and refused to wear

glasses, but in spite of this drew better than anybody in the school. The piano was beyond her.

Apart, however, from her accomplishments, her learning, her ignorance, and inability to be young, it was her story-telling that most astonished her fellow students. She evidently carried on *viva-voce* for their benefit her habit of romancing. This much, at least, she brought of her life at Haworth to Roe Head. There seems to have been a pause in literary production co-incident with her time at school. I have a notion Branwell's literary activities were less furious during her absence.

Branwell and she were very thick just now. He even paid her at least one surprise visit at school. She wrote to him every week in preference to the others.

"Dear Branwell,—As usual I address my weekly letter to you, because to you I find the most to say,"—on the subject of politics, extreme pleasure over the defeat of the Reform Bill, which extreme pleasure convinced her that "I have not as yet lost *all* my penchant for politics." She was just turned fifteen. In this interesting letter there is a patronizing reference to the "little wild, moorland village where we reside," a jab at Papa's ma-lingering and another at Aunt's reminiscences of the "salubrious climate of her native place."

The Parsonage, with its "growing potatoes," Aunt and Papa, evidently suffers by comparison with Roe Head. She has recovered from her homesickness.

One other letter of this year 1831 must be referred to. It is addressed to "Dear Miss Nussey," who is evidently on a half-term exeat. Therein Charlotte, with absurd formality, declines an invitation to a series of lectures on Galvanism, declines on the score of duty and diligence. The breach is widening between the "moorland village where we reside" and the world where lectures may be heard on Galvanic experiments.

It was not only the propinquity of Galvanism that ruined Charlotte for home, or home for Charlotte. There were other spirits of the age abroad that destroyed her peace of mind for ever and a day. There were spirits of unrest, social, religious, romantic. Moreover, Discovery and Enlightenment were busy at work—very disturbing things—and Improvement, the most horrible devil disguised as an angel of light that ever stalked up and down in the world and to and fro in it. And as thick as butter over everything it was the fashion to spread sentimentality.

Having been reared, as it were, in the end of the previous century, the Brontë children had not much use for sentimentality, but it blighted their vision, just as New Art blighted the vision of people twenty years ago, and—I do not know the current phrase—Robotism blights our own. In a future chapter there will be more to say on the subject of the lily of the valley and the dark eyes of Grecian Maids, symbolic of this blight.

What else Charlotte got out of Roe Head we know from *Shirley*. *Shirley* is the novel of its atmosphere, informed by its social spirit, brightened by many of its characters, beautified with its landscapes. This softening influence in Charlotte's life produced (forgive the

99

pun) her softest novel, for soft it is in more ways than one.

It has been declared that the heroine of that novel, "Caroline Helstone," is Ellen Nussey. Outside yes, inside no. It is a cunning trick by which Charlotte tried to disguise a flattering self-portrait. The name alone gives the game away. Charlotte—Caroline; Brontë—Helstone (hell-stone is a word for those lumps of meteoric iron which we connect with Thunderbolts), and Brontë is the Greek for "Thunder" according to Charlotte.[1] There is more than that to it of course. *Shirley* is full of Charlotte's conversations with Emily, as for instance the conversation about Cowper's poem *The Castaway*, a thing that meant a deal to Emily later on, and to Charlotte and Branwell also.

I will make two quotations from *Shirley* with direct reference to this time in Charlotte's life, merely to inspire the curious to study that book with a new interest.

Here is a description of how and why Caroline (alias Charlotte) came to get an education:

"Caroline had never known her mother, as she was taken from her in infancy . . .; her uncle, the rector, had for some years been her sole guardian. He was not, as we are aware, much adapted, either by nature or habits, to have the charge of a young girl: he had taken little trouble about her education; probably he would have taken none if she, finding herself neglected, had not grown anxious on her own account, and asked, every now and then, for a little attention, and for the means of acquiring such amount

[1] Charlotte called herself C. T. "Charles Thunder." Branwell she called "Patrick Boanerjes." She often played with the name Brontë.

of knowledge as could not be dispensed with. Still, she had a depressing feeling that she was inferior, that her attainments were fewer than were usually possessed by girls of her age and station."

Here is a description of Mary Taylor's home where Charlotte visited:

"This is the usual sitting room of an evening [the back-parlour]. Those windows would be seen by daylight to be of brilliantly-stained glass—purple and amber the predominant hues, glittering round a gravely tinted medallion in the centre of each, representing the suave head of William Shakespeare and the serene one of John Milton. Some Canadian views hung on the walls—green forest and blue water scenery—and in the midst of them blazes a night eruption of Vesuvius; very ardently it glows, contrasted with the cool foam and azure of cataracts and the dusky depths of woods."

Another blow at the moorland village—those Niagaras and flaming mountains!

Shirley is a strange book. It is tempered with discretion and verisimilitude—Charlotte's ideal autobiography. Take all the facts and details of a life, remove incongruous time and place to shake down the action, stir the facts and details about, guarantee that all will more or less come right in the end, lost mothers return, the heroines marry, put in no fictitious characters, and you have *Shirley*.

There is a job for a Brontë-lover some day to undo *Shirley* and put all the reminiscences in right sequence, and the characters in their right homes, to sort out the real references to Emily and the ideal references, and skin Ellen Nussey off Charlotte. It will suffice for the

101

moment to say that the Curates ought to be at Haworth, the French tribe more or less in Brussels. The rest will do pretty well where they are in the neighbourhood of Leeds and Halifax, Mr. Helstone excepted. He should be divested of a certain cheerfulness and popped back in the Parsonage with his dyspepsia.

When you have read this novel of hers, conceive of Charlotte's attitude toward her home, after she has had eighteen months in this politer world. There is a politer world in Yorkshire where the Moors do not intrude, where people, quite southern, may be found, not at all Wuthering Heightish; and there are valleys where peaches actually ripen sometimes on the walls and roses luxuriate in summer. Charlotte learned to love that kind of thing at school, and to love unbarbaric gentle characters, provided they were honest and had bones in their backs. Fortunately for her she had a good stiffening in her own body.

Gifted with extraordinary powers of observation, memory and insight into character, Charlotte is devoid to my mind of poetic insight. She cannot see the wood for the trees, cannot grasp the Grand Idea, she has not that male streak in her without which no woman is a supreme artist, was not hermaphrodite as the great artists are. Male singleness of heart and female one-with-earthishness—conception of Heaven, and oneness with life, these two things seem to me absent in Charlotte, but all of Emily. Heaven in this sense comprises hell; Life, the wind, animals, dark and light, actual

102

being as against knowing. Being Creation, and Knowing the Creator, that is the Grand Idea.

Charlotte was not on that scale. She was constructed on a perfectly comprehensible plan. What she might have become, had the octopus of education not strangled her natural impulses, it is hard to say. Most people become what they are after all. But the octopus of education is a terrible blood-sucker, a squeezer out of human juices.

XV

CHARLOTTE ENDEAVOURS TO ENLIGHTEN HER SISTERS

"If you like poetry, let it be first-rate; Milton, Shakespeare, Thomson, Goldsmith, Pope (if you will, though I don't admire him), Scott, Byron, Campbell, Wordsworth, and Southey. Now don't be startled at the names of Shakespeare and Byron. Both these were great men, and their works are like themselves. . . . Omit the comedies of Shakespeare and the Don Juan, *perhaps the* Cain *of Byron, though the latter is a magnificent poem . . . ; that must indeed be a depraved mind which can gather evil from* Henry VIII., Richard III., *from* Macbeth, *and* Hamlet, *and* Julius Cæsar.*"

Charlotte Brontë to Ellen Nussey, 1834

IT is a terrible thing what slaves we moderns are to book-learning. In the old days, scholars, pedagogues and priests went to school as others were prenticed to their trades. Now that we have lost our trust in God and man, we rely on algebra and Latin declensions to fit us for life. In some countries a dash of culture is added, how to tell Guido Reni from Raphael, Schumann from Schubert, and other unessential knowledge. In England only old maids bother their heads about that. I speak of ordinary people who do ordinary jobs in the world. Individuals look after themselves as they always did and will.

This pest of education has not long taken the nature out of our minds. In Charlotte's day, disease though it is, it shone with the light of a new dawn to the anxious and earnest. Now we begin to see that that light was the phosphorescence of putrefaction.

It was Charlotte's business to acquire as much education and culture as she chose for herself; neither yours nor mine. Unfortunately her generosity, to give it a good name, and inability to leave other folk alone, to give it a bad—made her take upon herself to inoculate Emily and Anne with the virus of education.

It is a curious thing that almost nothing got done in the Brontë family that was not set going by Charlotte.

Some women have an extraordinary force—a force of will that really removes more than mountains. It has got men out of Eden and gods out of Valhalla, set armies on the march and put armies to bed to be nursed. It is illogical, incongruous and usually quite blind. Hence its strength. Women who exert these powers as a rule do not foresee the widening circles of disturbance which their determination spreads. They concentrate a slow steam-roller force upon propelling their victims before them toward an immediate goal. They do not adjust the force to the event. Women will exert as much power to thrust a husband into a dress suit on a given occasion as they will to get the Pope from Avignon or put the heroes of Sevastopol into sanitary sickcots.

The only salvation from this frightful force is to run away. Women are called weak, but when they

105

arise in the strength of their endurance, the strongest man had best clout them on the head or fly. Otherwise he will surely die.

Sometimes I think it is real inorganic force—if such a thing can possibly be—that this kind of woman exerts. When she is good into the bargain, right, you know, wise with worldly wisdom—Heaven indeed help those about her.

These female titans would be the last people to claim this power—horrified if any knew their propensities for crushing, they are blind as bats in more ways than one, often submissive in manner and feeble in physique.

But enough of generalities.

Directly Charlotte got home from Roe Head she set up school over her sisters. "In the mornings from 9 o'clock to half past 12, I instruct my sisters and draw, then we walk till dinner, after dinner I sew till tea time, and after tea I either read, write, do a little fancy work, or draw, as I please. Thus in one delightful, though somewhat monotonous course, my life is passed."

By September, Charlotte writes—" . . . Consider the situation in which I am placed, quite out of the reach of all intelligence [news] except what I obtain through the medium of the newspapers." She is longing for the world.

She obviously feels definitely superior to Emily and Anne, separated from them by experience and knowledge. She is only sixteen, of course, a most superior age. Ellen Nussey and Mary Taylor, her "grown up" friends, are her standbys. It is hard to believe, reading

Charlotte's early letters, that William IV is still on the throne, that we are now in 1832, and not well in the middle of the reign of Queen Victoria and Prince Albert, but like many a man of mind, Charlotte was ahead of her time.

It was not only common knowledge that Charlotte brought back to her sisters at Haworth; she was accompanied by the Arts of Literature, Music and Painting.

She knew her Guido Reni from her Raphael, if not her Giotto from her Cimabue. She made meticulous imitation engravings from representations of the masters.[1] Music was beyond her practice owing to her poor sight, but a piano came shortly to the Parsonage. As for literature—Shakespeare, Byron, Scott, Hume, Wordsworth, Campbell, Cowper, Southey, Boswell's "Johnson," Moore's "Byron"—she had read or was reading these mighty personages.

I do not know what effect all this influx of learning had upon Emily. We know little about Emily's thoughts on literature or art.

The only three writers I can discover any feeling of hers about are Cowper, Rousseau and later—Hoffmann.

There are a couple of pages in *Shirley* on the subject of Rousseau and Cowper which are very interesting. There was one poem of the latter's which got the whole family by the ears—*The Castaway*. In this poem the

[1] Mr. Brontë supplemented Charlotte Brontë's artistic efforts and instruction with a few lessons from a Mr. William Robinson of Leeds, who taught Branwell portrait painting. Mrs. Gaskell says he was a man of "considerable talent but very little principle."

poor hero has been washed overboard, and in spite of "the cask, the coop, the floated cord" perishes within sight of his mates after an hour's battle with the waves. Cowper compares the Castaway's plight with his own:

> "No voice divine the storm allayed,
>   No light propitious shone,
> When, snatch'd from all effectual aid,
>   We perish'd, each alone!
> But I—beneath a rougher sea,
> And whelm'd in deeper gulfs than he."

One can see wherein lay the appeal to Emily.

In *Shirley* she is made to say: "One could have loved Cowper, if it were only for the sake of having the privilege of comforting him."

Charlotte gives many reasons forthwith why Cowper could not be loved, adding—"And what I say of Cowper, I should say of Rousseau. Was Rousseau ever loved? He loved passionately; but was his passion ever returned? I am certain, never. *And if there were any female Cowpers and Rousseaus, I should assert the same of them.*" (The italics are mine.)

"Who told you this? . . ."

" . . . The voice we hear in solitude told me all I know on these subjects."

"Do you like characters of the Rousseau order [Charlotte]?"

"Not at all, as a whole. I sympathize intensely with certain qualities they possess: certain divine sparks in their nature dazzle my eyes, and make my soul glow.

108

Then, again, I scorn them. They are made of clay and gold. The refuse and the ore make a mass of weakness: taken altogether, I feel them unnatural, unhealthy, repulsive."

And now comes the sentence that marks this conversation as a pitiful blind reminiscence of a painful moment in Emily's life.

"I daresay [answers Shirley] I should be more tolerant of a Rousseau than you would . . .: submissive and contemplative yourself, you like the stern and the practical."

One feels the reserve in this ghost of a conversation, feels Emily keeping back her own thoughts and sees that Charlotte knew not what she has made plain to us. Her opinion of Rousseau occupies her, Emily's silence occupies us.

No wonder; when she set to writing poetry, Emily kept herself to herself.

Of course for all her high reading and high thinking, poor Charlotte's eighteen months' education was very much that of "Stratford-atte-Bowe." You don't know what provincialism is until you get to Yorkshire. We admire scratchings in the way of Art that a suburban would scorn, and crack up poetry that the back page of a parish magazine would refuse to house—our own productions; but—and the but is enormous—for all our *naïveté* we have our grandeurs. Before the war you might have heard remarks such as this from a manufacturer to his wife:

"Maria, put me opery-'at in along o't' rest. I'll

be meeting t'nobs at Nijni!" Nijni-Novgorod, you
know. We have long been on familiar terms with the
dear old place. Our merchants used to go there to
barter knives and wool as a matter of course—and to
Leipzig and Milan.

Our sons were often educated abroad; my father, son
of a small shop-keeper, got his education near Weimar,
for instance.

That some of the fathers of Charlotte's friends or
of the children she educated had cosmopolitan connections is certain (Mr. Taylor, father of Mary, for instance), but they said nowt about it.[1]

She went herself to Brussels. Our wideness and our
narrowness were amazing—and so were Charlotte's.

I'll tell you this, we get more out of Niagara and
Vesuvius (*vide* the Taylors' back-parlour), and Goethe
and the Russian Empire than any of you know. These
things go to make our silence. We have no intellectual
appreciation of them but rather gather them up as part
of ourselves. In the old days, the West Riding of Yorkshire, narrow though it seemed to the casual foreigner,
spread deep and wide underneath.

I, even I, grandchild of an old fellow that kept a toy
shop, was kissed by Ellen Terry when I was a child,
in her dressing room, sitting on her dressing hamper in
Sheffield itself.

Which may seem irrelevant but is not. These things

---

[1] I believe Mr. Taylor spoke several European languages, and had
travelled considerably, but at home always used his "native Doric," *i.e.*,
spoke broad Yorkshire.

give us a self-respect—are a part of our grandeur—to hob-nob with the merchant princes of the world at Nijni, to be kissed by Ellen Terry. They agree very well with the moors that cradle us.

The Brontës may have been cooped up in a black highland village, but it was not only their genius which made them make a familiar of Wellington and the great, it was the genius of the country in which they were born.

With this background, it is pitiable to think of Charlotte teaching her sisters the bit of book-learning she had come by. They needed, Branwell, Charlotte and Emily, a fine, generous education if they needed any. That would have done Branwell and Charlotte no harm. Emily was *hors concours* from the start, unteachable, thank God.

XVI

ON BYRON AND BYRONISM

*"His dark eyes and swarth skin and Paynim fea-
tures suited the costume exactly: he looked the very
model of an eastern emir:—"*
Mr. Rochester in fancy dress in *Jane Eyre.*
Charlotte Brontë

AFTER the contradictions in the last chapter which
I shall leave as they are for your benefit, for your
ingenuity to unravel, I will continue to heap
up an accumulation of rubbish and other things, that I
may finally extract Emily from the middle of it in-
tact. There are several years of this heaping-up process
ahead, for it is still only 1832.

At the beginning of the century England had been
thrilled and frightened by the spectacle of a *Really
Wicked Man.* He had been defeated, dethroned, at the
battle of Waterloo. At that same battle his successor in
villainy, Childe Harold, had assisted as spectator. Childe
Harold was now also among the shades, but his ghost
walked. Disguised as Don Juan, he crept even within
the walls of Haworth Parsonage. What a ghost! As
handsome as a hero, as evil as the devil, irresistible to
the ladies, a Turk where females were concerned. A

112

Lord Byron   *National Portrait Gallery, London*

"THE DARK HERO"

splendid ghost for young romantics and sentimentalists, a *dark hero* of a ghost in fact.

Byron after death became at least six feet tall; if he limped at all, it was next to nothing, just a romantic hitch of one magnificent shoulder. His eyes were enormous, their dark glance full of fire like a stage dragon's. He had silken lashes of a length only to be met with fringing the eyes of tailors' dummies, and under the heaven of his dark curls, a mind—Dionysian is a polite adjective for the mind allotted to the gorgeous exile by tradition. This enormity was expelled from his native land for the sake of our innocent daughters, for the sake of decency.

Did Charlotte and Emily never give the wretch a thought? Did they never flirt with him outside the pages of *Don Juan?* Of course they had Moore's Life to correct the public portrait of him by. But Moore and Ethel Colburn Mayne have written in vain of his fatness and his shortness, and his sufferings and his lameness. The world does not want their Byron; it prefers its own, for the world is thrilled by the Dark Hero, and likes to see him proud and tall and magnificent in exile.

As I said before the Dark Hero is universal. Though he chooses in whom and when to become incarnate, he has a property in us all these days.

We shun the creature, but when he rigs himself out as conqueror or poet, worship him. We like the shiver he sends down our spines, and the thrill his lordship gives our nerves. We enjoy him at Black Mass.

Our Byron is so obvious, so cheap, so flagrant, we

113

cannot avoid setting him up in opposition to that effeminate long-haired Christ in the church window. There lies a hell behind the dark browed flagrancy and a heaven behind the fair-haired sweetness; in that Hell you will find others beside Fairfax Rochester and Heathcliff, the first an upholstered kind of devil to be sure, the last quite the genuine article.

I want to present the Dark Hero here with all the clap-trap of sentimentality. Sentimentality was rife in Emily's day. In spite of their robustness of mind the Brontë children did not altogether escape its taint. Sentimental symbolism was a curse of art and literature. The Ivy, Lily of the Valley and Violet adorn the virtuous, the Stag and Steed are at the service of the brave; ruins, Norman doors, cathedral aisles, mills, lakes and mountains form their setting. Shrieks, ghosts and nuns frighten the timid, large-eyed ladies into the arms of their bewhiskered knights.

Huge eyes, tapering waists and Grecian noses were essentials of beauty. People actually saw the masterpieces of Michaelangelo and Raphael (to judge from contemporary reproductions) got up in this style. How the eyes of the Madonnas rolled! With what straight noses did the engravers endow Adam and Eve!

Here comes Byron of the perfectly lovely head. He soon gets furnished with a perfectly lovely body. The painters do not tone down his curls or glance. He is dark and wicked to boot—and faithless—and a poet.

There is Emily at Haworth, exiled from love, with a man's soul in her female body, hell tormenting her, poetry adding to the torment. When she begins to express the poetry in her, is it unnatural or surprising that the hero of her dreams, King Julius, should have a dark and impious eye, that there should be more than a touch of Byronism in her Gondal poetry. After all he was the heroic villain of his day and it was Emily's day. Like will to like, though the one is a ghost dolled up in all sorts of extravagant rubbish, and the other a lonely child on a moor as ignorant as a rock.

So much for Byron's ghost. It is a vain enough bogey, not so vain in its symbolism though. Did not Emily perchance recognize behind all the fluster a brother in torment?

XVII

FAMILY GROUP

*"Alas! as lightning withers
The young and agèd tree,
Both they and I shall fall beneath
The fate we cannot flee."*
Emily Jane Brontë

IN the autumn of 1832 Charlotte went to visit her
dear and charming friend, Miss Nussey, in her
elegant home, Rydings near Birstall. Branwell took
her over. He called Rydings "Paradise." The Brontës
all had pretty much the same idea of "Paradise" as applied to mansions on this earth. Crimson carpets and
drapery, white mouldings picked out in gilt, crystal
chandeliers. I dare say Rydings provided these glories.
They "awed" Charlotte. Heathcliff never saw them
but through a plate-glass window. As a child in such
surroundings he would have thought himself in heaven.
Branwell must have glowed considerably to the two
at home over his first intrusion into the magnificent
world. Charlotte never lost her passion for crimson
rooms, in the end, she crimsoned the parlour at Haworth, many years later.

The following summer Miss Nussey came to Haworth. It is from her *Recollections* of this visit that

116

ANNE, EMILY, AND CHARLOTTE

most of these descriptions are drawn. Not all by any means though. The rest come obliquely from Charlotte's letters and *Shirley*.

Ellen Nussey found the Parsonage plain and bare, but its dove-grey rooms with the hair-seated chairs and walnut tables (not yet Victorian) had an air of refinement, almost of elegance.

The venerable Mr. Brontë, aged fifty-six, with white hair and a perfect wasp nest of a cravat, did the hospitalities with a high-bred courtesy. He was considered invalid. Charlotte was not inwardly fond of him, though outwardly a dutiful daughter. She would "rather be out of his presence than in it." He had the art of making himself agreeable to strangers, but in the bosom of his family he was stern and silent. "As he puts away his cane and shovel hat in the Rectory-hall, so he locks his liveliness in his book-case and study-desk: the knitted brow and brief word for the fireside; the smile, the jest, the witty sally, for society." He "is neither tyrannical nor hypocritical: he is simply a man who is rather liberal than good-natured, rather brilliant than genial, rather scrupulously equitable than truly just."

Ellen Nussey came in for his best half and, whatever she thought, was loyal to the man whose salt she had eaten. But Charlotte thought aloud under cover of *Shirley*.

The old man fired his pistols off from his bedroom window every morning, related the same old stories about terrific local people, preached extempore on a Sunday and showed a constant dread of fire.

117

When Mrs. Gaskell saw him years later, she found his conversation pompous, mixed with moral remarks and stale sentiments. Mrs. Gaskell hated him. She disliked Arthur Bell Nicholls even more (Charlotte's ultimate destiny), and from all she learnt of Emily, gathered only an unpleasant impression. I warn you Mrs. Gaskell had the violent dislikes of a vivacious, generous, rather indiscreet lady.

To return to 1833. The opposite chimney corner in the parlour was occupied by Aunt Branwell, an antiquated little lady now, airing her reminiscences of her gay youth and the "salubrious climate of her native place" for the visitor's benefit, and coquettishly horrifying her by presenting the gold snuff box. She, in the armour of her frightful cap, was not in the least terrified by her *vis-à-vis*, old Brontë, as I daresay Ellen was. She tilted arguments with him in a lively, intelligent manner concerning the books she read aloud to him and showed her independence generally.

Mrs. Yorke in *Shirley* wears Aunt Branwell's cap. Has she got Aunt Branwell's tongue? Did Charlotte never have the following argument with Aunt?

"I should be sorry not to learn to sew: you do right to teach me, and to make me work."

"Even to the mending of your brother's stockings and the making of sheets?"

"Yes."

"Where is the use of ranting and spouting about it then?"

"Am I to do nothing but that? I will do that, and

118

then I will do more. . . . I have said my say. I am twelve years old at present, and not until I am sixteen will I speak again about talents: for four years, I bind myself an industrious apprentice to all you can teach me."

It is fairly clear from Charlotte's correspondence that she did not like Aunt, but "showed her her duty," as the phrase was. Charlotte was far too well-bred, obedient and good ever to say anything outright against Aunt and Papa. The Fourth Commandment was still observed in her day, and the manners of the time governed the children's attitude toward their parents strictly.

It has been said that Mrs. Pryor of *Shirley* is descended from Miss Branwell. I cannot feel that that is so. The good elderly women of Charlotte's writings are more likely to be one of the Misses Wooler, I think.

Next in order about the tea table came Charlotte, "not grown a bit, but as short and dumpy as ever." To judge from her letters, her style of conversation was as elaborate as Papa's. Her hair had gone out of "frizz" into "window-curtains," but her clothes were still hideous. She refused to wear spectacles although she was half blind with short sight. Her terror was not fire, like old Brontë's, but strangers and strange animals, cows and things. Her mouth was firm and straight and determined, her nose ugly and too large. Papa kept his now faded handsomeness to himself.

She adored the Great Dead, still adored Wellington, loved Charles Wellesley and the Marquis of Douro

119

almost as much as ever, and hated among her contemporaries Cobbett. This is interesting. Cobbett stood for the good old days when a man's home was his castle, were it ever so humble. He was not set on women's education, and foresaw the blight the Industrial Revolution would cast upon our green country and the blight it and its congeners would cast over the national heart. Charlotte leaned the other way, Improvement, Enlightenment, Education. She liked polite modesty and admired gilt drawing-rooms, and in her heart put the reading of French before brewing and baking. "His principles (whether private or political)" were "no great favourites" of hers.

"When Adam delved and Eve span,
Who was then the gentleman?"

No, Charlotte had no sympathy with that sort of thing —but she taught in Sunday School.

Branwell came home to tea when there was a charming young lady visitor from "Paradise." He was going to be an artist and already daubed in boiled oils upstairs in the back room. The creatures of his hand glowed in the beauty of very pink flesh. They say he was already too often down at the Black Bull. It had not ruined his innocence yet, nor the family hope in him. He was writing busily in his spare moments of Verdopolis, and the family prognosticated a grand artistic career for him. When the girls went far afoot he accompanied them by his father's order, and when they went upon the moors, he ran in the van with Emily and Anne

120

and teased the other two over dangerous places. They, of course, Charlotte and Ellen, were quite grown up now. Ellen was deferentially called Miss Nussey by the young ones, now and always.

Branwell had quite enough of the old man. Papa taught him the classics and slept in the same room with him. He had not Charlotte's power of "perpetual recurrence" by which she got her way. The future was still theoretically his. Papa had a thought to make him a parson, but he did not seem to urge it.

Branwell and Charlotte still shared a literary life, but they did not share his merry village life, his bright friendship with the sexton, his games with the lads of the village. Charlotte was a womanly, shy little creature, bird-like—with that mouth and dumpy body and will of steel—and Branwell was a young man, though he didn't grow. It is manly to swear and fight and talk and parade as cock-of-the-walk even if you are barely five feet tall.

Next in order of precedence came Emily. "The cleverest o' t' Brontës," said the village—but then she could bake and iron—she was "more like a boy than a girl," they added. She could run on the moors. Emily had just gone fourteen. "She was the tallest person in the house except her father." She had a muddy complexion and dark hair, frizzed like a Hottentot's. "She had very beautiful eyes—kind, kindling, liquid eyes." Ellen Nussey never forgot her smile, a rare, infrequent smile. "Strength of self-containment" and power, that was her deepest memory of Emily. Out on the moors she became a light-hearted child; alone without the others apparently she came out of her shell and could be vivacious, but as a rule she talked very little and showed an "impenetrable reserve."

Occasionally on the moors, she used to philosophize, sit on a stone amidstream and chase tadpoles, and moralize upon the strong, the weak, the brave, the cowardly.

But there is much lacking in Ellen's picture of Emily. She does not ask why Emily was so reserved, how she had acquired that strength of self-containment.

She says that no serious sorrow had so far cast its gloom on Emily's youth. We at a longer date may feel it had.

Emily was not often very merry. As seldom was she angry. But when she did get into passions her features became not distorted, but fixed. She scarcely looked angry, only resolute, and in haste; yet one felt that an obstacle cast across her "path would be split as with lightning." Charlotte told Mrs. Gaskell that when Emily's face whitened and her mouth set, when her eyes glowed in her pale face and she compressed her lips to stone, no one dared to interfere with her.

For the most part she held herself silent and aloof, feeling and knowing things, while Charlotte saw and recorded many matters.

Sometimes Charlotte tried to break down that reserve, but she got no change out of Emily.

Emily had a strong love for animals as lonely people sometimes have. In animals they find the faithfulness and sympathetic constancy that they miss in men.

122

Animals can be their own. They see in them noble characters which they find not elsewhere. A dog can become very dear to a lonely man, a real friend.

There was only one dog in those days at the Parsonage, very much kept under by Aunt. Emily and Anne shared their breakfast with him.

We all know what it is like when a sister's "dearest friend" comes to stay with the family. However charming and sociable the friend may be, there is a strong proprietary protectiveness exerted by the sister. When the friend comes from a superior world as Miss Nussey did, the others feel inferior while the sister is showing them off. They blossom out a bit on their own when left alone with the dear one, and in those sports and games in which they excel show off quite a little for her benefit.

One day, it is said, to the surprise of everybody Emily volunteered to take Ellen Nussey a walk alone while Charlotte indulged in a headache. Charlotte was apparently on the usual tenterhooks that strain the nerves of sisters with dearest friends. When the pair got back she said to Ellen, "How did Emily behave?" Emily behaved her best, glad of this enlivening natural stranger, the first she had ever met in her life—but Charlotte said, "How did Emily behave?" Those words make one feel quite cruel. If I had heard her say them of me I should have wrung her neck, or like a fool, have gone into the back yard and wept, for the glory would have departed from that happy afternoon.

Of course there was Anne at the Parsonage, Anne of the violet eyes and pretty complexion and big nose. I always forget her, though Emily and she spent hours and hours together.

One feels that the family was divided into pairs in these days, Charlotte and Branwell—Emily and Anne. Soon Emily and Anne will set up a literary rivalry against Charlotte and Branwell. Anne is just a child. She shares Emily's secret thoughts no more than the others. For hours a day she still sewed at Aunt's knee. She had very bad colds. That complexion of hers was suspiciously pretty. But she could run still on the moor, nevertheless, and hugged the doctrine of Universal Salvation morbidly to her breast.

There is no more to be said of Anne now.

The family group is complete. All are at home. It is summer weather. The old clock ticks in the hall, the sun sets late. Flush of day hangs in the north all night. There is peace and calm and cheerfulness at Haworth. When the hour of sleep comes, Charlotte and Emily and Anne take their guest upstairs to the Den. There is no good-night at the door. They all crowd in it seems, all four of them, unless Emily goes and sleeps with old Tabby as she did on occasion. Branwell paints in the only spare room, Aunt and Papa have the two big front apartments, I can only suggest that perhaps Anne joined Aunt. I hope so, but I doubt it.

Ellen Nussey was Charlotte's closest friend. She had her confidence, and deservedly. Everybody liked her.

124

Emily, Anne, Aunt, old Brontë, Tabby in the kitchen. Yes, I think she was always Charlotte's closest friend, more than any of the family. I think at this time Charlotte loved Ellen more than she loved the others, though she came later to feel a heart-breaking love for Emily. Emily's reserve hurt Charlotte, I am sure. She must have wanted a closer relationship; to be able to sympathize, to console, and alas, to guide. It is quite clear Emily kept Charlotte off. One can imagine she tried at times how far she might show herself safely to her sister, and have been warned by experience not to disclose too much. Lucy Snowe would have tried to manage Heathcliff.

One must recollect that in these days Charlotte was at the silly age, the age of self-importance. It is not her fault that the limelight must be turned upon her at her worst and at her best. Most of us are, fortunately, insignificant and at school during the coltish years. She was at home making her place with Emily, and not succeeding very well.

Emily admired her. She certainly did bring new interests into the family. Emily listened to her and felt the strength and honesty of her opinions. It is not uncommon for brothers and sisters to want other members of the family to know and love their souls, and yet to be aware how much those souls would be disapproved of. They hide their souls away, therefore, and recognize the difference between being loved and liked, and love but do not like in return. One can recognize and

125

admire another's character without feeling the slightest kinship with it.

There are many points of contact between two intelligent sisters in the same family, especially when both have enthusiastic natures. Though they may differ in their enthusiasms, the one catches fire at the other. As the years went on Charlotte damped down her wildness, her romantic enthusiasm (self-confessed) with stern self-lecturing, with the aid of duty, decency and a sense of inferiority; but in her youth at home, she was not altogether the self-repressed little smouldering volcano that she afterwards became, a volcano that by sheer power of will supplied itself with a steam gauge and safety valve that worked indifferently well.

The whole trouble seems to have been that Charlotte and Emily were of entirely different calibre. Emily was a genius after all, and Charlotte tremendously talented.

It is a very subtle and difficult thing to give an idea of the relationship of these two sisters. No matter how many letters we had or opinions or descriptions, we should still fail to possess evidence whereby to estimate the exact degree of familiarity between them. There are such fine shades of feeling, so much—I use the word telepathy—between them,—the telepathy of familiarity that does not survive in letters and other people's recollections.

I have gone into Charlotte's character at some length and tried to record her feelings toward Emily at this time and shall try to record them again, because Charlotte was the main-spring of the family life at Haworth.

We owe to her the Duke of Wellington and his sons, Ellen Nussey, Brussels, the publication of six novels and probably the energy of starting their creation. Some people think we owe the conception of Heathcliff to her and a good deal more. It has even been madly suggested that she wrote *Wuthering Heights*.

XVIII

EMILY AND ANNE

"If grief for grief can touch thee,
If answering woe for woe,
If any ruth can melt thee,
Come to me now!"
                 The Appeal, Emily Jane Brontë

"My life is very lonely,
My days pass heavily,
I'm weary of repining;
Wilt thou not come to me?"
                 Appeal, Anne Brontë

ELLEN NUSSEY had scarcely left Haworth before Emily fell very ill of erysipelas in the arm; she had a bad attack of biliousness and became generally in a very poor state of health. A wet and miserable winter succeeded the pleasant summer, and an unusual number of deaths took place in Haworth.

Altogether it was a melancholy season, that winter of 1833-1834. There was nothing new apparently at Haworth and I will take this leisure, therefore, to enquire as far as I can into the relationship of Emily and Anne.

It is quite certain during this time that Charlotte and Branwell were playing their old literary games together. What were Emily and Anne up to, inseparable in their

128

From a drawing by Charlotte Brontë

EMILY BRONTË

leisure moments? Had they any interest in the life of Verdopolis in which Captain John Flower, M.P. (Branwell) and the Honourable Charles Albert Florian Wellesley (Charlotte) took such delight?

If Emily or Anne wrote anything before 1836 it has been lost or destroyed or sunk in the anonymity of the *Young Men's Magazines*.

If they played without writing what did they play? Anne's nom-de-plumes later on are Lady Geralda, Alexandrina Zenobia and Olivia Vernon. Emily's only nom-de-plumes that I know of are R. Alcons and the signatures J. A. and A. G. A.

Charlotte used her own name or that of Lord Wellesley, Branwell his own, or John Flower, or John Bud.

When Wellesley began to write of Angria and the verdant beauty of its tropic clime, did Anne and Emily decamp to Angora, as cold and savage a spot as imagination can provide? There to their hearts' content in later days, they are their Geraldines and Alexandras and Juliuses and Douglases versus the Marians and Henriettas, Adrians and Percys of the other two.

I lay stress on these names:

Angria—Angora.
Zamorna—Zalona.
Adrian—Julius.
Percy—Douglas.

Most certainly Emily and Anne were copy-cats. Angora seems to have been a crib, if not a rival of Angria, Angria turned sour however. They both are torn with wars and revolts as time goes on.

Now the last literary effort with an Angrian title is *Percy: A Story*, by P. B. Brontë, 1837. Soon after then, at any rate, the Angrian literature came to an end.

The first Angoran or Gondal poem of Emily's we have is on a manuscript dated 1836, and Anne's first preserved manuscripts are dated 1836-1837. The Gondal Chronicles do not begin until 1841.

Charlotte's *My Angria and the Angrians* is dated 1834; the Gondal Chronicles were written between 1841-1845. *The Life of Field-Marshal the Right Honourable Alexander Percy, Earl of North Angerland, by John Bud*. P. B. Brontë is dated 1835, the Life of King Julius, by Emily Brontë, was begun in 1845.

I will not seek to deny that Angora or Gondal imitated Angria considerably, but it seems to me from these slight indications that it was set up in imitation, not in concert, and probably after the other two had taken to literature more seriously.

I will defer consideration of Emily's private sufferings as Julius, King of Angora, until a later date when that monarch begins to express himself in verse.

To come back to 1833 and the next year. There is no direct evidence at all that Emily and Anne were at play. Ellen Nussey noted that they were inseparable companions and spent much time walking up and down arm in arm. Were they talking Angoran nonsense then? Did the Lady Geralda confide her woes to the strong bosom of A. G. A., as she leaned upon his arm? Were these two not wanted by Lord Wellesley and Captain Flower?

Who knows?

Younger members of the family are often a trial to their elders and betters. I may point out that one of the names used by Anne, "Zenobia," is that of a protagonist in one of Charlotte's early stories. There is some likelihood that the younger pair carried on the games invented by their elders, long after Charlotte and Branwell had discarded them. Charlotte wrote of Zenobia as early as 1829. This is all mere theorizing, and very weak from want of evidence.

Because Anne was no poet, and her novel *Agnes Grey* is dull to boredom, because Charlotte and the rest have ever called her "dear gentle Anne," she has survived to posterity as a pale, clinging wraith. Why was this gentle creature Emily's inseparable companion? Were they thrown together because they had no other friend of their hearts, and being thrown together clung to each other even as two strangers who have nothing in common will hobnob on a desert island?

Anne had not Emily's natural power of self-expression; on the other hand her mind was not now or hereafter overlaid with Charlotte's culture. She was in character, "milder and more subdued; she wanted the power, the fire, the originality of her sister, but was well endowed with quiet virtues of her own." "A constitutional reserve and taciturnity placed and kept her in the shade." Added to this she had endurance where Emily had energy, says Charlotte.

Reserved and taciturn and in the shade, these words seem dark enough to suit Emily in a mournful mood.

131

Is there anything in Anne's poetry to suggest what made her so?

> "When sinks my heart in hopeless gloom,
>   And life can show no joy for me;
> And I behold a yawning tomb,
>   Where bowers and palaces should be;
>
> "In vain you talk of morbid dreams;
>   In vain you gaily smiling say,
> That what to me so dreary seems,
>   The healthy mind deems bright and gay.
>
> "I too have smiled, and thought like you,
>   But madly smiled, and falsely deemed:
> *Truth* led me to the present view,—
>   I'm waking now—'twas *then* I dreamed."

There is another poem beginning: "O, God! if this indeed be all" and ending "Then call me soon to Thee; Or give me strength enough to bear My load of misery."

There is sufficient evidence, of which these poems are but a fragment, that Anne was of a melancholy nature. She refused, as Emily refused, human consolation. The only consolation that could soothe her soul was Faith in God. The spirit of Faith was her comforter.

In a long poem addressed to *The Three Guides,* we get a fairly complete insight into Anne's mind. It was written long after this date when Anne had well made up her mind about spiritual matters. It is her philosophy, her *Philosopher* Poem, in fact.

First therein she addresses the spirit of Earth, by which

I gather she means common sense; secondly, the spirit
of Pride:

> "Spirit of Pride! thy wings are strong,
> Thine eyes like lightning shine;
> Ecstatic joys to thee belong,
> And powers almost divine.
> But 'tis a false, destructive blaze
> Within those eyes I see;
> Turn hence their fascinating gaze;
> I will not follow thee!"

In answer to which the spirit replies that she may
"Cling to the earth, poor grovelling worm"; and concludes his tauntings thus:

> "There's glory in that daring strife
> Unknown, undreamt by thee;
> There's speechless rapture in the life
> Of those who follow me."

She replies that she has seen his votaries with his
lightning in their eye, his triumph on their brow.

> "Bold and exultant was their mien,
> While thou didst cheer them on;
> But evening fell,—and then, I ween,
> Their faithless guide was gone."

What shall they do when night grows black, they who
before were sustained by Pride o'er the mountain's
brow?

She knows him and will have no part in him, but

chooses Faith to bear her up toward a Heaven of Hope and Peace and Love.

Anne certainly saw the Dark Hero, and knew the Three Gods that waged war in Emily's bosom. We do not expect transcendentalism of her nor genius, but she has been dismissed too hastily in the past from Emily's company.

Emily and Anne have gentler things in common than brooding melancholy and silence. They love flowers. "The Bluebell is the sweetest flower," says one; "My childhood's darling flower," says the other. "There is a spell in purple heath," sings Emily. Anne rhymes "dreamy spell" and "heather-bell."

These are small matters, but loving-kindness is largely made up of small matters. Anne recalled all these things when she was far away from home.

> " 'Tis strange to think there *was* a time
> When mirth was not an empty name.
>
> "When speech expressed the inward thought,
> And heart to kindred heart was bare.
>
> "And all the joy one spirit showed
> The other deeply felt again."

Anne and Emily had one great virtue in common. They did not study their thoughts and actions in the light of the world's approbation.

When Anne was writing *The Tenant of Wildfell Hall*, a much underrated book, Charlotte says "she hated her work, but would pursue it." She felt it her duty to warn others with this book of the terrible effects "of talents misused and faculties abused." "When reasoned with on the subject, she regarded such reasonings as a temptation to self-indulgence. She must be honest: she must not varnish, soften, or conceal. This well-meant resolution *brought on her misconstruction,* and some abuse, which she bore . . . with mild, steady patience." Charlotte regarded the choice of the subject as a "*mistake,*" an "*entire mistake.*"

Both Emily and Anne said what they had to say without considering the squeamishness, the approbation or the pleasure of the Public. So did Charlotte in her first book, but she was sorry for it and did not err in that way again. She kept her honesty within decent bounds.

Of *Wuthering Heights* Charlotte says, "Whether it is *right* or *advisable* to create beings like Heathcliff, I do not know: I scarcely think it is." She finds an *apologia* necessary to the world for his existence.

There is no need to comment on the words I have italicized. The difference between Charlotte's attitude and that of Emily and Anne is quite clear.

XIX

THE FAMILY BREAKS UP

"Emily is going to school, Branwell is going to London, and I am going to be a governess. This last determination I formed myself knowing I should have to take the step sometime, and "better sune as syne," to use the Scotch proverb; and knowing well that papa would have enough to do with his limited income should Branwell be placed at the Royal Academy and Emily at Roe Head. Where am I going to reside? you will ask. Within four miles of yourself, dearest, at a place neither of us is unacquainted with, being no other than the identical Roe Head mentioned above. . . . Emily and I leave home on the 29th of this month; the idea of being together consoles us both somewhat."

July 6th, 1835, Charlotte Brontë to Ellen Nussey

ON July 29th, 1835, Charlotte and Emily went to school at Roe Head, Charlotte as governess at £16 a year, Emily as a pupil.

We know nothing about this period of absence in regard to Emily except what Charlotte tells us in her preface to the *Selections from the Literary Remains of Ellis and Acton Bell.*

Emily failed to endure the disciplined routine of school. "Her nature proved here too strong for her fortitude. Every morning when she woke, the vision of home and the moors rushed on her, and darkened and saddened the day that lay before her. . . . Her white

136

face, attenuated form, and failing strength threatened rapid decline."

Charlotte says she felt Emily would die unless she returned home and obtained her recall. "She had only been three months at school; and it was some years before the experiment of sending her from home was again ventured on."

In connection with this time at school Charlotte gives among the Selections three poems of Emily's "crude thoughts of the unripe mind, the rude efforts of the unpracticed hand," written in Emily's sixteenth year.

Charlotte makes a number of misstatements in this account. To begin with, Emily was full seventeen when she went to Roe Head, secondly, "the experiment of sending her from home" was ventured on by Emily herself or others, about eighteen months after she left Roe Head. True, she went as teacher, not as pupil. Thirdly, the "rude efforts" of her unpracticed hand, to wit, *A little while, The Bluebell is the Sweetest Flower*, and *Loud without the wind is roaring*, are dated December 4th, 1838, December 18th, 1838, and November 11th, 1838, respectively.

I know of no dated poem of Emily's earlier than July, 1836.

While Charlotte was at Roe Head, she sickened herself and fell ill of an acute attack of morbid religious mania. If her account of Emily's sufferings were not corroborated by similar sufferings under similar circumstances, I should have felt it too erroneous to take much stock

137

of, partly because of her actual misstatements of fact, and partly because persons in her then state of mind see things in a very queer light.

There is another point. Charlotte edited these poems of Emily's with a heavy hand and altered them. May she not have edited and altered Emily's sufferings at Roe Head? It is romantic to pine for the moors, not quite so romantic to weep and turn white with resentment because you have been made to do something against which your soul revolts.

Why should Emily turn white against the kindly discipline in force at Roe Head? I feel we have to go a long way back, to Cowan Bridge and the Death Room episode. Prison—that is the word that comes to mind. The moors are not prison. They typify escape and freedom. It is not for the moors that Emily pines, but prison that she hates, and restraint that she resents. "Nobody knew what ailed her but me—I knew only too well." I do not think for a minute Charlotte really did nor could know what ailed Emily. She almost knew, but not quite.

What Charlotte attributed to homesickness was due to incarceration, a kind of claustrophobia, I think, a prison complex. One would have expected something of this sort to happen. It has happened and it happens again.

This time, fortunately, Emily was released after only three months' torture. By the end of October she was home again.

Many thoughts arise about this business. Did Charlotte want to make Emily less uncouth, more learned, ladylike, or to fit her out to be a governess? Did she feel it only fair that Emily should enjoy the same improving advantages as herself (as she did later), or feel that Emily, too, ought to prepare herself for the necessity and duty of earning her own living? The Dark Hero is to be improved, must turn governess. He is already a general servant, but to work with his hands never degrades him.

Charlotte evidently failed to console Emily by her presence at Roe Head, or to reason her into a sensible frame of mind. They did not see life with the same eyes, their views were incompatible. Again one feels how widely separated these two sisters were, and suspects that Charlotte's attempts to order Emily's behaviour, though well-meant, must have made worse rather than relieved her sufferings; for every exposition of the virtue, necessity or expediency of an attitude contrary to the attitude of revolt, only makes the rebel feel an added weight crush him down, an added bolt put upon the prison door. It is no use to show that the bonds are light, the durance a privilege. The durance is vile in the Dark Hero's heart, and not even if Archangel Michael himself turned warder, and the rules were as few as those in the Garden of Eden, could he support it. He is a prisoner, others order his life with rules meaningless for him. There is an end of the matter. He turns white and moans for whatever freedom he knows, and at the first opportunity makes off.

139

XX

CHARLOTTE AND BRANWELL WOULD BE POETS. EMILY BECOMES ONE

"I trust I shall never more feel ambitious to see my name in print; if the wish should rise, I'll look at Southey's letter, and suppress it."
Charlotte Brontë to Robert Southey

EMILY seems to have spent the whole of the next year, 1836, at home. Charlotte was at Roe Head getting worse of religious mania, and Anne had gone back with her instead of Emily. Branwell has been to London on an abortive visit. He went there with a view to gaining admittance to the Academy Schools. He did not stay long, and came home depressed and disappointed, but he saw the sights, including Westminster Abbey and Tom Spring, the prize fighter, and his powers of entertaining the patrons of the Black Bull were enhanced thereby. He was always going down to the pub when any guest from the outer world dropped in.

Apart from the absence of Anne and Charlotte, life wagged on. Emily did not teach in Sunday School as Charlotte did, nor play the organ badly like Branwell. There was a piano at Haworth Parsonage now which, perhaps, gave her some pleasure. Ellen Nussey had a high opinion of her playing, even before she went to Brussels.

On July 12, 1836, Emily broke into verse. This verse really is immature. There is nothing much to be said for the four pieces which we have of hers belonging to the rest of this year. Suffice it to say that two of them are mythical (probably Angoran) pieces, and that her thoughts already intertwine darkness and glory.

At Christmas Charlotte came home again. She decided to become a poet, which resolution Branwell took at the same time. He had long been convinced that he was an author and had written more than one letter to his beloved *Blackwood's Magazine*. He had long known he was "not one of the wretched writers of the day." Nevertheless the editor of *Blackwood's* would not understand the advantage of securing his assistance to support the magazine.

On January 19, 1837, Branwell wrote to Wordsworth, politely informing him that "when there is not a *writing* poet worth a sixpence, the field must be open, if a better man [e.g., P. B. Brontë] can step forward." Wordsworth's reply, if any, is not known.

Just about the same time, Charlotte wrote to Southey for literary advice. Her letter, according to herself, was a "crude rhapsody." Southey took three months to reply to the "senseless trash" of an "idle, dreaming being." She had, he said, "what Wordsworth calls 'the faculty of verse.'" "Literature," he warned her, "cannot be the business of a woman's life, and it ought not to be."

Charlotte stuck to her guns. When once this remarkable woman got an idea into her head, she *could not* get it out.

In the meantime, in the early months of 1837, where was Emily? What was she doing? Anne was still away at school. If, therefore, Emily was at home, she was at home alone, and in no happy mood.

In time we shall know what other poems Emily wrote in these months, now I can tell you of only one:—

> "Redbreast, early in the morning,
>   Dark and cold and cloudy grey,
>   Wildly tender is thy music,
>   Chasing angry thought away," etc.

That is all very well. Though the robin's song set her writing, her angry thoughts were not chased away. The poem was obviously written in a mood when thought is swifter than the pen. She began it quite calmly, continued it in a mood of self-pity, and ended up with a shriek.

> "I heard it then, you heard it too,
>   And seraph-sweet it sang to you;
>   But like the shriek of misery
>   That wild, wild music wailed to me!"

Emily was, in a fair way, to become a poet.

In the middle of this poem of a hurt and angry mood, a little child strays from its father's cottage door and lies lonely on a desert moor. There you have the lonely child theme mixed up with angry thoughts developing

142

into a shriek. It is clear that the analysis of the cause of all this anger was a means of recruiting that anger. Self-pity is the grand recruiting ground for the devils of resentment.

What caused the resentment that produced this very personal poem? I do not know.

Four months later, on June 10th, Emily wrote a curious poem on the subject of seeing things at night. A shadowy ghost comes to her at evening and curdles her blood with "ghastly fear, and ghastlier wondering." "It seemed close by, and yet more far than this world from the farthest star" parted from her not by space or time but by "the sea of death's eternity, The gulph o'er which mortality Has never, never been."

Between now and December Emily wrote, inclusive of this poem I have quoted from, six bad-dream or nightmare poems, very complete and, for her, long. The spectre comes at evening again: his call, "whistles round the gloomy wall" as he haunts the lonely child one drear winter's night. Another time slumber moulds the poet's misery into a strange spectral dream, whose phantom horrors revealed to her the "worst extent of human woe." It begins with a cry:—

> "O God of Heaven! The dream of horror,
> The frightful dream is over now."

This is August 7th.

On October 14th she sets out to write a Gondal Poem, it breaks off after five verses into a bad dream, and becomes

"An undefined, an awful dream,—
A dream of what had been before."

In November she wrote *Sleep brings no joy to me*
and *I'll come when thou art saddest.*

Listen! 'tis just the hour
  The awful time for thee:
Dost thou not feel upon thy soul
A flood of strange sensations roll,
Forerunners of a sterner power,
  Heralds of me?

These six poems are by far the best ones she wrote
during those months, in fact, the other fifteen are either
only fragments or of not much account.

The lonely child theme is mixed up with the nightmare theme.

"Those tiny hands in vain essay
To thrust the shadowy fiend away."

"Darling enthusiast, holy child,
  Too good for this world's warring wild;
  Too heavenly now, but doomed to be
  Hell-like, in heart and misery."

" 'Dreams have encircled me,' I said,
  'From careless childhood's sunny time.' "

"The waste of youth, the waste of years,
  Departed in that dungeon thrall;
  The gnawing grief, the hopeless tears:
  Forget them, oh, forget them all!"

144

"Sleep brings no joy to me,
Remembrance never dies."

"A memory, whose blighting beam
Was flitting o'er me evermore."

December is chiefly given over to Gondal Poems: there are three to hand. The subject of two is death. My death, whoever I am. In one occurs this line:—

"Mother, come near! my heart is breaking."

The year winds up with a personal poem, *To a Wreath of Snow,* a "voiceless, soul-less messenger" whose presence waked "a thrilling tone" that gave her comfort.

"Methinks the hands that shut the sun
So sternly from this mourning brow
Might still their rebel task have done,
And checked a thing so frail as thou.
They would have done it, had they known
The talisman that dwelt in thee."

It is Christmas again, a year since Charlotte wrote to Southey. Emily has become a poet. The Dark Hero has begun to express himself. What set him off? Why this nightmare? What woke awful memory? Against whom the resentment? None of the poems of this year have any calibre but the frightful ones, many of these others, indeed, run to but a few lines, some end in the middle of a line.

In this year Emily has experienced horror. Why? I leave it at that.

145

XXI

AN ACADEMY FOR YOUNG LADIES

"For many a week and many a day
My heart was weighed with sinking gloom,
When morning rose in mourning grey
And faintly lit my prison-room."
December, 1837.   Emily Jane Brontë

ON August 24th, 1837, Charlotte wrote to Ellen Nussey, who was then at Bath:—

"I have nothing at all to tell you now but that poor Mary Taylor is better, and that she and Martha are gone to take a tour in Wales."

This letter is headed Dewsbury Moor, to which place Miss Wooler had moved her school. In a subsequent letter Charlotte wrote to Ellen Nussey who was apparently still at Bath:—

"The Taylors have got home after their Welsh tour."

Her other news is that "Emily is gone into a situation as teacher in a large school of near forty pupils, near Halifax. I have had one letter from her since her departure; it gives an appalling account of her duties—hard labour from six in the morning until near eleven at night, with only one half-hour of exercise between. This is slavery. I fear she will never stand it."

146

This letter is dated by Mrs. Gaskell October 2nd, 1836; by Mr. Clement Shorter April 2nd, 1837. It obviously ought to follow that of August 24th, 1837. Let us give it the provisional date of October 2nd, 1837, a very likely one.

Between August 24th and October 2nd Emily presumably, therefore, went as school teacher to a school near Halifax, Miss Patchett's academy for young ladies at Law Hill.

The Brontë family never seems to have taken any step in life without endless discussion, endless airing of the pros and cons. This is the only undertaking of any of them to which there does not cling some remnant of tiresome planning and family argument. Even over such unimportant matters as visits of Ellen Nussey, we get these phrases: "Aunt thinks it would be better if you deferred your visit until" such and such a time "because ——"; "Aunt wished me to give you this information before, but papa and all the rest were anxious I should delay. . . . I myself kept putting it off from day to day"; and so forth and so on, a maddening state of affairs.

There is no other reference to this absence of Emily from home than the one I have quoted in Charlotte's letters now available, nor in her prefaces or reported reminiscences. But for this letter and a few words of Ellen Nussey's, "Emily was a teacher for one six months in a ladies' school in Halifax or the neighbourhood," we should not know that she had ever held such a post.

147

As to whether Emily went a-teaching of her own free will or not I leave you to make what deductions you think fit from this and the preceding chapter. Recollect that she suffered this year, particularly on and after June 10th, from nightmare, that memory reawakened. Whose were "the hands that shut the sun So sternly from this mourning brow"? Why was she angry and resentful as early as February? What were the "Relentless laws that disallow true virtue and true job below"? And who promulgated these laws about July 26th? A host of questions.

Christmas came in due time and Emily, of course, rejoined the family for the holidays. They were not a cheerful crowd. Charlotte was still in a morbid frame of mind. She had had a downright row with Miss Wooler about Anne's health. Dewsbury Moor did not suit Anne. According to Charlotte, she showed every sign of consumption. Miss Wooler evidently thought Charlotte fussy, and after a scene promoted by Charlotte, in which that young woman reduced her headmistress to tears, Miss Wooler wrote home to Papa saying that Charlotte had taken her to task. Papa ordered the girls home, and home they went at once, not, however, before Charlotte and Miss Wooler were reconciled after a fashion.

Anne continued to ail over Christmas and Charlotte remained in a terrible state of nerves. Ellen Nussey was invited to stay, and Charlotte had built upon the promised visit for weeks beforehand. Alas! one cold and icy evening Tabby, their old faithful servant, fell down in the street and broke her leg, and very nearly died of the consequences. Directly she was able to be moved, Aunt wanted to have her sent to a sister who lived nearby. Papa agreed, but the three girls, it is said, struck and refused to eat until the elders allowed them to take on the nursing of poor Tabby. As they were not able to get a new servant immediately not only had they to nurse Tabby, but largely to do the work of the house.

Ellen Nussey's visit was put off. "It seems," wrote Charlotte, "as if some fatality stood between you and me. I am not good enough for you, and you must be kept from the contamination of too intimate society. . . . Should Tabby die while you are in the house, I should never forgive myself. . . . All in the house were looking to your visit with eagerness."

Charlotte could hardly live without Ellen in these days: presently she even contemplated marrying Ellen's brother, whom she did not love, to have her friend always living with her. Needless to say she did not succumb to that temptation.

In due course Charlotte went back to Miss Wooler at Dewsbury Moor, leaving Anne behind. Did Anne carry on the nursing of Tabby and the extra housework alone? On January 4th Anne was much better, but still required a great deal of care. Was she strong enough by the end of the month to undertake this charitable labour?

Whether Emily went back to Miss Patchett's after Christmas, or whether she stayed at home to assist with

149

Tabby, I cannot say. She was at home by June 7th.

We have another dungeon-poem beginning "Weaned from life and flown away In the morning of thy day," followed by a Death poem and another referring to the fearful vision. By March we are done with nightmare. Last year this was the inspiring theme: this year, 1838, Gondal begets almost all her poetry. Until November at least she fails whenever she starts off to write a personal poem. I say she fails because these little poems run to no more than two lines or a stanza.

"There are two trees in a lonely field,
    They breathe a spell to me;
A dreary thought their dark boughs yield,
    All waving solemnly."

"What is that smoke that ever still
Comes rolling down that dark brown hill?"

" 'Twas one of those dark, cloudy days
    That sometimes come in summer's blaze,
When heaven drops not, when earth is still,
And deeper green is on the hill."

These are perfect descriptions of queer Yorkshire weather when the land seems bewitched with silence, ominous silent weather, when the colours of earth become unearthly, and the stillness seems impossible in a living world. These poems were written in June when Emily was certainly at home, and Charlotte was home from Dewsbury Moor, having all but had what is called a complete nervous breakdown, the culmination of her religious fever aggravated by contemplation of the worst doctrines of Calvin.

I will take occasion to say here that Charlotte found teaching almost as unendurable as Emily. She never did nor could understand or like children. Never again does she hold a job for more than a few months. I have a strong suspicion that she returned to Dewsbury Moor after the summer holidays, which is contrary to the general impression, but she certainly had done with it by Christmas. For years, however, she tortured herself and unintentionally her family, with the necessity of teaching, but nothing came of it, save that Anne, and odd though it may seem, Branwell presently went governessing.

During the summer of this year Charlotte's friends the Taylors, Martha and Mary, came to stay at the Parsonage. Heaven knows where they slept. Mary was, to Charlotte's mind, in consumption. That did not prevent them having a right merry time, playing the piano, talking their heads off. Strange are the ways of fate! Mary outlived Charlotte, Martha died young. The Taylors seem to have been the most intelligent and lively friends the Brontës ever had.

Perhaps it was on this visit that the religious discussion took place, reported by Mary Taylor. "One time I mentioned that some one had asked me what religion I was of (with a view of getting me for a partisan) and that I had said that that was between God and me. Emily (who was lying on the hearth-rug) exclaimed,

151

'That's right.' This was all I ever heard Emily say on religious subjects."

It is strange that Emily was home in June if she were still engaged to Miss Patchett. Whatever months were school holidays, June was certainly not. Also it is strange that we have more Gondal remains belonging to this year than any other if she were away from Anne. Beside those poems in Mr. Shorter's *Complete Poems of Emily Jane Brontë* (1923), there is a longish Gondal narrative called *The Wanderer*, dated from Bradford.

Bradford? Why Bradford? If she were at Miss Patchett's what was Emily up to at Bradford?

"Uncle" Morgan seems to have been at Bradford in this year. Branwell rented a studio in Fountain Street, Bradford, during the autumn at least, where did he live or lodge? Was Emily a guest at Uncle Morgan's for a while, or did she by any possible chance housekeep for Branwell?

In November Emily certainly appears to have been from home, "drear and lone and far away": the title of her poem *The Wanderer* is echoed in a line of one poem dated November 1st, 1838. Says the poet to the wind:—

". . . Where, wild blast, dost thou roam?
What do we, wanderer, here, so far away from home?"

Then we get on November 11th:—

"Grim walls enfold me."

On December 4th [1]:—

> "A little while, a little while,
>   The noisy crowd are barred away."

And on December 18th:—

> "If chilly then the light should fall
>   Adown the dreary sky,
> And gild the dank and darkened wall
>   With transient brilliancy."

Now, Law Hill School was situate in a small village on a hill. These quotations suggest a town, such as Bradford, rather than the little village of Southowram with its open prospect six or seven hundred feet above sea level.

If she were chained up at Law Hill, I should not have expected her to be at home during the school term in June, nor should I have expected an outbreak of Gondal poetry to adorn this year.

A suspicion haunts me that the three famous poems of *Loud without the wind was roaring, A little while* and *The Bluebell* are final versions of some earlier verse. We know that the first stanzas of *Loud without the wind was roaring* are rewritten from a fragment dated 1836. These three personal poems in a Gondal year are singularly finished and complete. Were they begun years before and rewritten in the gloom of a Bradford winter?

Though the years 1837 and 1838 are hidden in clouds, though the scavengers have ably destroyed almost all evidence of these months, one thing is clear to me be-

[1] Date furnished to me by C. W. Hatfield, Esq., from the Houresfeld MS.

153

yond all question. In these hidden months Emily suffered, and in her suffering conceived that revenge which filled *Wuthering Heights*.

In point of fact, however, it is only certain that Emily was home in June, at Bradford some time, and home for good by the following April. I surmise that she was at home for the best part of the year, nevertheless. Perhaps time will disclose what happened at home, at Bradford, or in the "dark prison house" on the moor. I can but re-assert that something very serious befell Emily, some event took place with grave results to herself, some time during the years 1837 and 1838. It is during this time that she began to write of betrayal and vengeance. Shortly afterwards begin the poems of guilt, of shame, of crime and of tarnished name.

XXII

GONDAL. A DREAM-DRAMA

" 'Dreams have encircled me,' I said,
'From careless childhood's sunny time;
Visions by ardent fancy fed
Since life was in its morning prime.' "
Emily Jane Brontë

ONE reason for my surmise that Emily was at home for the best part of 1838 is that, as I suggested in the last chapter, in that year there was a great output of Gondal poetry. Without the Gondal literature which has been destroyed, it is waste of time to attempt to reconstruct the Gondal dream-drama, a ten years' dream of two people, many of the "facts" of which, if one may call them so, were imitated from the immensely long dreams of two other people.

Plays of this nature have certain characteristics which are common not only to themselves but to the work, taken as a whole, of many imaginative writers, perhaps of all imaginative writers. The main sources of inspiration will be found in the private history of the dreamer. (I shall speak now as if Gondal were the entire work of Emily, which in one mood it certainly was its deepest mood.) Setting aside all psychoanalytic theories of the origin of dreams, it is not necessary here to go behind the conscious in seeking for the spring that releases the creative impulse. Conscious hate, conscious inferiority, conscious love, conscious jealousy, any of these feelings will suit my purpose which is to show not what the Gondal Saga was, but how unlikely it is that until that dream had made itself a shape in the long course of time there was any saga in any sense at all.

Most imaginative artists never arrive at the saga stage reached by Balzac and Zola. Dostoevsky, Melville, and Shakespeare never hammered out their experiences into anything resembling consecutive order. They appear in their own works simultaneously under different circumstances and with different names. I say simultaneously because the major event, episode or experience behind say half a dozen of their creations was one and the same. Ibsen declared that his complete work was the history of his experience, that his plays must be read consecutively in order to understand the whole progress of his thought. Yet even so Ibsen appears personally in *Rosmersholm*, which in either the strictest saga sense or the sense of real life would make it impossible for him, having thrown himself in a mill-race, to appear on the scene again. How, then, could he logically reappear in *Hedda Gabler* and *Little Eyolf*, which he undoubtedly did?

If a man kills himself off in any of his creations, one may be reasonably certain that he will in different situations, which may be the situations of the moment, go

156

through the torture that led up to his suicide again and again, and survive or die of it tentatively. Few enough have early in life killed themselves off for good in their own creations as Emily Brontë and Rimbaud and Melville did.

However, if a man kills himself off in his imagination in any of his writings, the mainspring of his creative impulse will very probably be found in the theme of that writing. No man slaughters himself even experimentally without the utmost provocation. When a writer ends his life for good, as Emily did hers in *Wuthering Heights,* it is almost certain that the theme of the book in which the desperate deed is done will be the major theme in the remaining work of that same writer. I speak in terms of consciousness all the time at present, of jealousy, of love, of hate and ambition in the most ordinary sense. Passion, betrayal, subjection, revenge and usurpation are the main themes in *Wuthering Heights.* *I assert that they were the main themes of Emily's lost Gondal writings,* wild inhuman passion, revenge and usurpation, revenge against more or less innocent persons.

Wuthering Heights has a curious characteristic that, as far as I know, is peculiar to itself. The main story of passion is told twice over. The first story ends in death, the second in life and happiness; but the first is *what happened,* the second *what might have been,* given the absence of revenge and usurpation. If at this late stage the dream can be repeated twice in two different aspects within the bounds of one short book, in how many

157

forms did it not appear and reappear in the ten preceding years of its existence, in the formative years of its existence as a dream-drama? Dozens and dozens, nay hundreds, of times in these dream-dramas, one experience gives rise to an episode of varying character. Take the theme of revenge, for instance. The avenger will slay his enemy, be slain himself, or not accomplish his end under the same circumstances upon the same occasion, or in different circumstances on many occasions.

Although the early imaginative creations of Emily were called by her the Gondals, do not for a moment imagine that it would be possible for us to compile a history of these Gondals, even if we had all the manuscripts. The only document with any coherence is possibly the missing *Life of King Julius,* one-half of which contained, I imagine, the surviving incidents of a ten years' game, and the other half of which was created on the spot out of the memory of past private emotions that King Julius had experienced on her behalf, or she on her own behalf. The story would be in the main that which had agitated her for the past ten years, and that which half a year later appeared under the title of *Wuthering Heights.*

For me the interest of the missing Gondal papers would lie in the elements of *Wuthering Heights* certainly to be found therein; their importance, in their being probably a unique though partial record of an actual dream-drama. When *The Wanderer* is presented to the public, we shall know a good deal more about the Gondals than we do now. For the moment we must do without it. But the more documents we had, the more confused the history of the Gondals would probably appear. To begin with, there would be two sets of documents, those chronicling the Gondal game as played with Anne, and those chronicling Emily's private Gondal dreams. The first set of documents would show descent from the Angrian game of Charlotte and Branwell, the second, the history of Emily's personal emotions. It is these that would contain the theme of *Wuthering Heights* more essentially. Had we those two sets of documents, we should then probably find that King Julius conquered and lost Elbë on the same occasion, until he definitely did one or the other in the *Life,* that he attained his happiness and did not attain it in love, and a thousand other contradictions. Episodes like *Douglas's Ride* and *Glenedin's Dream* would probably remain in mid-air.

Speaking of *Glenedin's Dream,* that poem itself contains an example of the double experience. Glenedin dreamed he slew the "princely victim" and also foresaw that himself the avenger fell, this deed of vengeance unaccomplished. Some logic exists between the two aspects of the episode in *Glenedin's Dream,* as it does in the two aspects of the story in *Wuthering Heights,* but no logic of this ordinary sort trammels as a rule the various versions of one episode in a dreamdrama.

Take a very common instance. You or I dreamed in our youth that we obtained a million pounds. In

159

dream one, a forgotten uncle of vast wealth dies in Australia and leaves it to us; in dream two, we make it ourselves in speculation; in dream three, we marry an heiress. There are many other ways open to the ordinary man whereby he may acquire, in dreams at least, vast wealth—for what? For the gratification of his desire for power, power to do good, to outshine his neighbours, in a word, to cease to be a humdrum individual and to become something of a hero.

By a strict sequence of ideas I have passed from the complexity of the dream-drama to one of its central and underlying facts. I am on the borderline between the conscious and the unconscious. You and I know we are not heroes endowed at birth with power. We dream that power comes to us in the shape, maybe, of a million of money. Once endowed from an outside source with power, then we feel we can act. But the gratification we experience in our dreams is not so much felt in the exercise of our power as in the moment of acquisition. You may think I am wrong, but four-fifths of our dreams will circle about the instant of acquisition, the other fifth more weakly describe exercise of our imaginary power. Oh, the sweet agony of the birth of the hero in us, that instant, to speak plainly, when imagination presents us with the cash!

But poets and their kind know they have power. The hero is born in them some time about the dawn of consciousness. They dream not of the acquisition of power, but of the defeat or victory of a power they already possess. That is, if the hero within them is the

160

Dark Hero. Not all poets have been Satan or Prometheus, destroyer and disintegrator of creation. All great poets before the Renaissance were princes. Since then poets have been princes also, and continue to be princes in our time, but they are not such by Divine Right as formerly. Our princes claim power in their own right. They boast an unknown origin like the popular heroes of old and sever themselves from men by this mystery of their beginning.

From this height descend to Haworth. In that place of "mists and moorlands drear, and sleet and frozen gloom," the Prince of Darkness had taken up his abode in a young girl. This girl was subjected to the narrow code of female behaviour in vogue in 1838. She was set below a brother with fair hair and had to serve this brother and his family in the capacity of drudge.

In 1846 this girl wrote a book about a place called Wuthering Heights, " 'wuthering' being a significant provincial adjective, descriptive of the atmospheric tumult to which its station is exposed in stormy weather." When the heroine of this story is "hardly six years old," about the time of the dawn of consciousness, there comes to her a Dark Hero of unknown origin who, for aught anybody knows, might have been the son of the Emperor of China, who at any rate is *"fit for a prince in disguise."*

The matters which chiefly concern this Catherine-Heathcliff personality are three. Catherine desires worldly prosperity and reciprocal passion; Heathcliff

161

desires reciprocal passion and revenge. Catherine tries to find both her desires from other sources than her Heathcliff-half. She betrays her Heathcliff-half to obtain both. Heathcliff seeks primarily reciprocal passion, but knows that he can only find it in his Catherine-half, and she betrays him to the world and tries to betray him to a fair lover, but she fails in that. The tragedy of *Wuthering Heights* is the tragedy of Catherine's inability to understand that love is obtained by self-surrender and not by dominion. Having failed to make Edgar Linton, who has already surrendered to love, understand that she wants him to force her to surrender to him, she falls back on Heathcliff, and these two indulge in a worship of themselves and a cursing of themselves the like of which was never seen before or since.

But Heathcliff has this other matter of revenge which urges him to destroy. To destroy what? First and foremost, that fair-haired Hindley Earnshaw, his foster-brother, by whom he had been made a drudge, who possessed Wuthering Heights when he, Heathcliff, possessed nothing. In the second place, he seeks to destroy that world for which Catherine betrayed him, and finally allows his unearthly passion for himself to destroy his own soul and body. Before his death, Heathcliff succeeds in usurping all Hindley's rights and in obtaining dominion over Catherine's world.

Such is a short summary of the essential features of *Wuthering Heights*, the book in which Catherine-Heathcliff comes to an end, body and soul, the book in

162

which Emily Jane Brontë kills herself off, body and soul.

As far as Emily is concerned, here is the summary also of the essential features of the Gondal dream-drama. Between the facts of Emily's real life and the story of *Wuthering Heights* that dream lies. Since it is a real dream, unhindered by possibilities and probabilities, all the facts are magnified to the utmost limits of the imagination. The prince figures in the dream, as a real prince, armies instead of machinations of one mind support him in his war of usurpation. The persons with whom he wars are princes, princesses, dukes, lords, and ladies. Wuthering Heights or Haworth Parsonage becomes a palace, Gimmerton Chapel or Haworth Church becomes a vast cathedral. In one poem, *North and South*, Gondal is apparently used outright for Haworth. In this poem blows that wind, that wild blast, that "atmospheric tumult," that "ocean-wind," that "Gondal wind" which haunts Emily's verse and prose, that "moor wind" which brought life-giving death to Catherine Earnshaw.

In this cold, wild northern place a prince suffers the utmost agony that a soul can undergo. On the whole his name appears to be King Julius. Very probably he is also Douglas, perhaps he had other names. Sometimes he appears as a "mournful boy" who becomes in time a "mournful man," an "iron man." How many forms this man took in his dream-drama stage it is absolutely impossible to say, but he finally appears as Heathcliff

163

in *Wuthering Heights,* bearing all the marks of a character that has long been in the world.

Heathcliff is well-known to the author of "Wuthering Heights" before the first word is written, as indeed are various other characters in the book, but the others were to be found walking about in the world, whereas no eye but Emily Brontë's had ever seen Heathcliff. *She* knew him as she knew herself. Heathcliff bears the stamp of imaginative maturity. His emotions in *Wuthering Heights* are not felt there for the first time, and the same may be said of Catherine's. The terrific force of *Wuthering Heights* had been gathering itself together for long enough. As thunder growls often for days before the final storm, so the passions in *Wuthering Heights* had growled for years. One fine outburst there was as early as 1838, a Gondal thunderbolt of passion almost as bright and flaming as Heathcliff's and Catherine's rage of passion just before she died.

This poem, *Light up thy halls,* contains not only Heathcliff's fury against Catherine for betraying him and herself, but also the curses which he and she shouted at one another in their agony.

"Oh! could I know thy soul with equal grief was torn,
    This fate might be endured, this anguish might be borne."
    .   .   .   .
"Say that *my* pangs are past, but *hers* are yet to come."

It contains the haunting of Heathcliff by Catherine after her death.

"Thine eyes are turned away—those eyes I would not see:
Their dark, their deadly ray, would more than madden me."

The last lines of this poem foreshadow the last words uttered by Heathcliff in this world, when he had prepared his vengeance and was ready to demolish the world he had won.

"Unconquered in my soul the Tyrant rules me still;
Life bows to my control, but *Love* I cannot kill!"

I cannot tell whether Julius or Douglas was the hero who slew himself and cursed his betrayer in this poem. It may have been another. There it stands at the beginning of the crime-poems, the poems of betrayal, which subject inspired Emily to write at least thirteen poems in the ensuing five years. Something very desperate must have befallen Emily in soul or body during 1838.

Since I have no more of value to say of Gondal, I shall take leave of it. Its myth is inextricably intertwined with Emily Brontë's actual emotions. I cannot disentangle it, nor do I believe, even if we had the whole Gondal literature, all that part of the myth shared with Anne, the story of the Palace of Instruction, of the struggle of the Royalists, the tale of Douglas, of Rosina, of Alexandra, of Arthur, and the rest of them, that it would be possible to separate her Gondal emotions from her own. Over and over again she seems to take to herself the suffering of her heroes. Of a dead Gondal she once wrote:

"What have I dreamt? *He* lies asleep,
   With whom my heart would vainly weep:
   He rests, and *I* endure the woe
   That left his spirit long ago."

Gondal is a true dream-drama, and like all such, its origin lies in the secret sufferings and desires of the heart that dreamed it, and its myth is the history of the thousand aspirations and sorrows of that dreaming heart.

XXIII

"CHILDE ROLAND TO THE DARK
TOWER CAME"

"Dark falls the fear of this despair
On spirits born of happiness;
But I was bred the mate of care,
And foster-child of sore distress.

"No sighs for me, so sympathy
No wish to keep my soul below;
The heart is dead in infancy,
Unwept-for let the body go."
At Castle Wood. Emily Jane Brontë

1839 was an exciting one at Haworth. In March, Charlotte received a cold-blooded proposal of marriage from Ellen Nussey's brother. In that gentleman's diary we have the following entries:

"On Tuesday last received a decisive reply from M. A. L.'s papa; a loss, but I trust a providential one. . . . Write to a Yorkshire friend, C. B."

March 8th, 1839. "Received an unfavourable reply from 'C. B.'"

Before October he was accepted by L. G.!

On April 8th Anne went as governess to a Mrs. Ingham, which episode in her life is embodied in *Agnes Grey.*

167

Before June, Charlotte tried to be a governess in a private family, that of Mrs. Sidgwick of Stonegappe near Skipton, cousin to Archbishop Benson. She was not satisfactory. She did not appreciate the Sidgwicks, nor they her. When one remembers that to their family belong our Bensons and our Sidgwicks, it seems strange they should have got on so ill together. We have two letters of Charlotte's from there to Emily, "Dearest Lavinia," containing an appeal for "raiment now manufacturing" and a long grumble. "Don't show this letter to papa or aunt, only to Branwell," she begs. The other letter, "Mine bonnie love," is a short few words of an exasperated soul.

Her letter to "My dearest Ellen," ending "Goodbye, *dear, dear* Ellen," when compared with these two, shows how Ellen had her closest confidences, her most intimate feelings.

By July 26th, Charlotte was home and Branwell returned from a thrilling visit to Liverpool. He wanted father, aunt and the whole family to go to this entrancing place of ships. Charlotte wanted to go to Cleethorpes with Ellen, a proposal made by Ellen that almost drove her "clean daft" with joy. Oh, dear! For six weeks or so the family wrangled over Liverpool versus Cleethorpes, whether Charlotte should go or not go, or all set out for Liverpool. I may say that after endless talk of "how" and "why" and "wherefore not" Charlotte went to Bridlington with Ellen and the rest of the family stayed at home. Charlotte cried when she saw the sea for the first time.

In the middle of all this pother there came to Haworth the first of the famous curates. He came to tea one day, did Mr. Bryce of Dublin University, fell in love at sight with Charlotte and proposed within a week. He, too, was sent about his business.

Most of this year Charlotte seems to have been in an irritable mood, easily put out, but Emily was from beginning to end in the very depth of gloom. First, in January, she mourned the downfall of her companions in the dark future, the tears that would be wept by the glad eyes around her, then bemoaned Anne's absence on April 15th in Gondal strains. In May she wrote two versions of another Bluebell poem also to Anne, followed by the fearsome personal poem beginning:

"I am the only being whose doom
   No tongue would ask, no eye would mourn."

In June she wrote *The Outcast Mother* (also called *A Farewell to Alexandra*). In July a Heathcliffian individual shows his face as an unknown guest with eyes of basilisk charm. A few days afterwards Emily writes *Come hither child, who gifted thee*, the poem I call the Fit Poem. Four days before her twenty-first birthday comes *Shed no tears o'er that tomb*. The year 1839 bore the first fruits of the horror that was past.

On August 30th there was a poem of loneliness in the Parsonage Garden, and then, we have a Song, bitter and cynical, which I think was addressed to Charlotte. Charlotte was just returning, or had just returned, home from Bridlington. Emily sang:—

169

"Oh, between distress and pleasure
    Fond affection cannot be!
Wretched hearts in vain would treasure
    Friendship's joys when others flee.

"Well I know thine eye would never
    Smile, while mine grieved, willingly;
Yet I know thine eye for ever
    Could not weep in sympathy.

"Let us part; the time is over
    When I thought and felt like thee;
I will be an ocean rover,
    I will sail the desert sea.

"Isles there are beyond its billow:
    Lands where woe may wander free;
And, beloved, thy midnight pillow
    Will be soft unwatched by me.

"Not on each returning morrow,
    When thy heart bounds ardently,
Need'st thou then dissemble sorrow,
    Marking my despondency.

"Day by day some dreary token
    Will forsake thy memory,
Till at last, all old links broken,
    I shall be a dream to thee."

Did a quarrel ensue?

There was a time, she said, when her cheek burned at scornful words, when she refused to curb defiance. Once

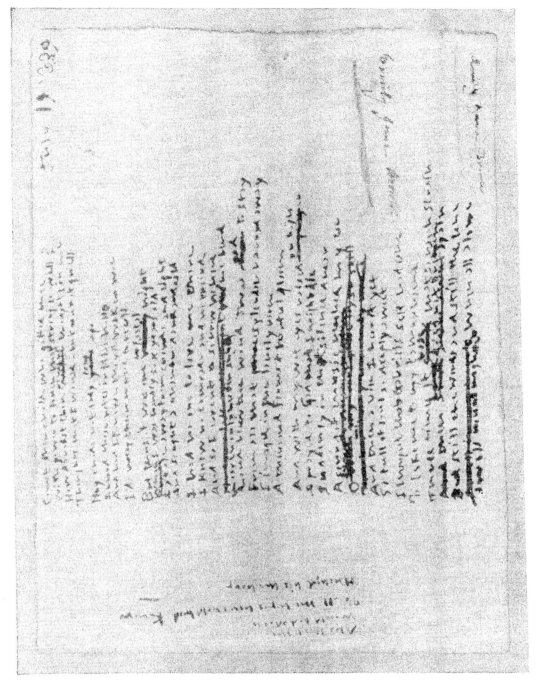

"COME HITHER, CHILD"

Facsimile of the poem I call the "FIT Poem." From a photograph made for C. W. Hatfield, Esq. by the late Henry Houston Bonnell, of Philadelphia, of the original manuscript in Emily's handwriting. Note the hitherto unpublished lines by Emily in the margin.

she would have died for truth, right and liberty, now she calmly bears deriding fools, not because she is tamed, afraid or ashamed. Her soul still chokes at selfishness and "self-clouded error," but she knows now that such wrath is useless. Howe'er, she frowns, "The same world will go rolling on." She referred again to her altered hardened spirit a little later, and in *Stanzas to* —— on November 14th, pitied some "wretch," "slave of Falsehood, Pride, and Pain," who was metaphorically (?) dead and buried. Amongst the few other poems of the late year there is one of extreme interest beginning:—

> "Come, walk with me; there's only thee
> To bless my spirit now."

A strong appeal is made to "friendship, dear and true." The friend replies, that friendship once perished cannot be revived, "And surer than that dwelling dread, The narrow dungeon of the dead, Time parts the hearts of men."

Somebody's spirit went away on a winter's night, some one departed "to the grave in youth's bare woe."

It seems to me that this was the year—Emily was of age, twenty-one in July—in which Childe Roland to the Dark Tower came.

XXIV

CUPID VISITS HAWORTH DISGUISED AS
A CURATE

"I'm afraid he is very fickle—not to you in par-
ticular, but to half-a-dozen other ladies."

"I am up to the dodges and artifices of his lord-
ship's character."

Charlotte Brontë, in letters to Ellen Nussey

CHRISTMAS again.

Poor old Tabby had to go to her sister in the end with that leg of hers. Anne had given up her situation with Mrs. Ingham. The ardent Mr. Bryce was dead.

But there came to Haworth and the district two curates neither of whom were distinguished for holiness, a Mr. William Weightman of Durham and a Mr. Collins presumably of Dublin. I very much fear that Mr. Collins is the Mr. C——, a curate, whose vices his wife knew were utterly hopeless. Mr. Brontë advised her to leave him for ever. Mary Taylor called him a hideous man. Charlotte wondered how a decent woman could ever have married him.

I do not want posthumously to blacken this gentleman's character, but I must, for Branwell's sake, suggest that there is a strong likelihood that Anne remembered Mr. C—— when she wrote *The Tenant of*

172

Wildfell Hall. May not this creature also have served Emily when she sent Hindley Earnshaw to the Devil in *Wuthering Heights?* Mrs. C—— came to the house. Is it likely her outpourings were confined to papa's ears alone? For they all knew the poor lady victim of "her wretched husband's drunken, extravagant, profligate habits."

Mr. Weightman was a young man of very different sort, a fair, handsome youth, a merry man, a man of wit and winning ways. He was Mr. Brontë's own curate, not a female heart within range but received a dart that struck home from his bright eyes. Haworth did not abound in beautiful youths. Ellen Nussey came to stay soon after his arrival. He spent hours at the Parsonage, sent the girls valentines and had his portrait taken by one of the artists there. The young ladies called him "Celia Amelia."

One night they attended a lecture of his at Keighley and were escorted home in the dark by Mr. Weightman and a married clergyman. The party was out till midnight. One gathers that this "assiduous" treader of toes was at his best during the long four miles on the dark highway. Branwell had gone tutoring at Broughton-in-Furness, so Mr. Weightman had the field to himself. Ellen Nussey at least had heart-stirrings on his account. As long as Charlotte remained at home, there was a deal of Mr. Weightman in her letters. Far and wide he spread his conquests to Swansea even, where he went for a time. Alas Cupid with his generous, open disposition and sweet temper—with all his "tricks, wiles

173

and insincerities of love"—could not long tolerate the gloom of Yorkshire; he stayed but long enough to excite all the female hearts he met, and forsook the body of poor William Weightman in October, 1842. Mr. Weightman died in "agonizing suffering," attended by Branwell, who had become extremely attached to him. Charlotte and Emily were then in Brussels.

I have gone to some length over this portrait of "Celia Amelia" Weightman who was so kind to the poor and so charming to the ladies, because he was the only man whom Emily seems to have found in the least agreeable. Ellen Nussey says he was the only one among the curates to whom she was even polite, but when he was making merry with Charlotte (in conversation), she would stay and listen and smile. Aunt, who tried to act as chaperone, was "precious cross" these days by the way.

While Emily was enjoying the society of Weightman, receiving valentines, and perhaps getting her toes trodden on beneath the tea-table, her poetry worked up to a wild state of grief. Nightmares were over, the wanderer had come home—to anger, death and guilt. The only person who had died was that Curate Bryce, who was, it seems, but once at the Parsonage, in the middle of the past year. I hardly think all these laments are wreaths for his grave.

The first two poems of the year are pitched in a Gondal key. Some Gondal hero has passed away. Says Emily:—

"I will not name thy blighted name
Tarnished by unforgotten shame."

But in the last verse of this particular poem, *Far far away is mirth withdrawn,* March, 1840, she took this hero's sufferings to herself.

> "What have I dreamt? *He* lies asleep,
>   With whom my heart would vainly weep:
> *He* rests, and *I* endure the woe
>   That left his spirit long ago."

Four poems of a poor sort on death and love, and one Gondal fragment are all that I know belong to the middle of this year. I think Charlotte must have done much recruiting for her anthologies out of 1840. She took *The Night Wind,* written on September 11th, also probably some of the undated Poems at the end of Mr. Shorter's collection of 1923 were written at this time.

As in due course there may be a new complete *Poems* of Emily Jane Brontë available, perhaps then it will be possible to fill in the gap. *Now*—it is not possible except by guess-work. I prefer not to guess on the whole.

In the meantime Emily's first poem of the year, *Thy sun is near meridian height,* gives me the text for a mournful review of her Poems of Guilt.

To go back: In April, 1839, Anne had gone away to earn her living. On April 17th "Arthur" purchased by his fall "Home for us and peace for all," and a few days later the poet, lying upon the moor, contemplated an unregenerate, hardened man, and cried "Oh! crime can make the heart grow old Sooner than years of wearing woe." In May the poet looked into his own soul and found corruption there. In July he ceased to pity one "shut from his Maker's smile." In October he bemoaned his altered hardened spirit. In November mourned some one's "ruined hope" and "blighted name." Then in a few fragments he lamented a departed youth. At the turn of the year in a terrible fit of melodrama the poet cried:—

> "Go, load my memory with shame;
> Speak but to curse my hated name."

and soon afterwards repudiated himself, presumably, in these words:—

> "I will not name thy blighted name,
> Tarnished by unforgotten shame."

A whole year later a ring discovered in some grass recalled his crime to him, and presently he bewailed the injury he had done his innocence. In October of the same year, 1842, in an introspective mood he again referred to his tarnished name, which mood revived in February. Back to the old theme he reverted in March, 1844.

> "I know that I have done thee wrong,
> Have wronged both thee and Heaven."

This poem and the long collection of Gondal verses, dated May, 1844, and the undated personal poem, *Honour's Martyr,* refer to untrue deeds and deeds of treachery.

176

"To aid a spirit lost in crime
I have no hope but thee.

"Yet, I will swear no saint on high
A truer faith could prove;
No angel from that holy sky
Could give thee purer love."

Thus spoke the Reckless Man, and thus cried *Honour's Martyr*.

"So foes pursue, and cold allies
Mistrust me, every one:
Let me be false in others' eyes,
If faithful in my own."

Behold the poet had made a virtue of his crime of five years' standing, and having turned his faithlessness upside down it became to him the finest faith under Heaven. His cursed name meant nothing to him now.

"I'll not give my inward faith
My honour's *name* to spare!"

He sang his crime no more.

In what shall we seek the source of these thirteen poems of five years, which I have plucked out and put in sequence? [1] In Anne's sacrifice of herself to work and Emily's refusal to leave home? Surely it was more than that. That some strange remorse for some strange deed, imagined or performed, tortured Emily's peace seems very clear—I leave it there.

[1] See Appendix IV.

Intertwined with all this woe are the love-poems, mostly feeble things. After the splendid Gondal poem of eighteen months before, wherein the Dark Hero raged magnificently, it is a poor fall to encounter in May, 1840, during Weightman's reign *The Appeal*. There follows in the next years some sickly stuff about a ring and a portrait. There was somebody with locks of light who looked a last adieu into the eyes of a young woman with raven hair. Some one with blue eyes gave a gentle kiss, penance and tender tears followed. This vapid thing seems to have found an early tomb. Emily is rarely at her best when she writes of the fair lover— especially when he takes on mortal guise. As for the death of this pale-haired milksop, shall we lay his corpse at Willy Weightman's door? Had some fond kiss of his set Emily sighing sentimentally? I daresay. The poems of guilt rise to melodramatic heights after his arrival, given new life perhaps by the aching of a heart, not for this young man, but for the true, fair, heavenly lover of whom he was but a hint.

XXV

ALONE WITH THE MOORS

"This is my home where whirlwinds blow."
Emily Jane Brontë

I WILL leave now guilt and love and let them rest. In real life it was 1840 still. Branwell was at Broughton-in-Furness. The muse has prompted him to badger Hartley Coleridge, and Charlotte has tried to write a novel about which she bothered Wordsworth, under the pseudonym C. T.,—short for Charles Thunder, I imagine. She is quite gay with the old gentleman. She was quite gay all that year. Poor Weightman cheered *her* up at any rate with his nonsense.

By September Branwell has quit tutoring and gone to be clerk to the Leeds and Manchester Railway. His friends were many in these days and ranged upward from Little Nosey, the landlord at the Bull, to Leyland the sculptor, and as mere acquaintance to give an air to a heterogeneous lot, Hartley Coleridge. Branwell was a very gay young man these days.

It is irksome to have to leave this cheerful brother and sister and stay by Emily in her tower of loneliness. She is so lonely that even the night wind expostulated with her, the wind that had been her friend from child-

179

hood. Wait until death to be alone, sighed the wind, I shall have time then to mourn you, and you *time to be alone.* Ha! Ha! There is almost a frightful joke in that. Ha! Ha! It is no use. Emily passed the winter apparently in black solitude and when February came wrote *The Caged Bird,* followed immediately by a poem of desolation which has hitherto been printed as part of *The Caged Bird.* I quote both in full.

> And like myself lone, wholly lone,
>   It sees the day's long sunshine glow;
> And like myself it makes its moan
>   In unexhausted woe.
>
> "Give we the hills our equal prayer:
>   Earth's breezy hills and heaven's blue sea;
> I ask for nothing further here
>   But my own heart and liberty.
>
> "Ah! could my hand unlock its chain,
>   How gladly would I with it soar,
> And ne'er regret and ne'er complain
>   To see its shining eyes no more.
>
> "But let me think that if to-day
>   It pines in cold captivity,
> To-morrow both shall soar away
>   Eternally, entirely free.
>
>   *   *   *   *   *   *
>
> "Methinks this heart should rest awhile,
>   So stilly round the evening falls;
> The veiled sun shows no parting smile,
>   Nor mirth, nor music wakes my halls.

"I have sat lonely all the day,
  Watching the drizzling mist descend,
And first conceal the hills in grey,
  And then along the valleys wend.

"And I have sat and watched the trees,
  And the sad flowers,—how drear they blow!
Those flowers were formed to feel the breeze
  Wave their light heads in summer's glow.

"Yet their lives passed in gloomy woe,
  And hopeless comes its dark decline,
And I lament, because I know
  That cold departure pictures mine."

You see what it is like within the Dark Tower?

Is your curiosity sated at last: soon you shall know with what ghosts Childe Roland peoples that gloomy haunt. Not yet awhile. Without its walls howls the wind, around stretches a barren moor. He may leave that fearsome place to visit the scenes of his human life, but he will not come back, not to this world, never again, in soul. He is doomed, most surely doomed; in the end he rids himself of his human body, the thing that takes him back to men, the thing that would not die. *He makes his body die,* and free, goes out to solitude where by the Grace of God mayhap the moor wind blows about his ghost, and the heather undisturbed feels the gossamer footsteps of his shade.

Meanwhile the moor comes upon Childe Roland a-crying. "Shall earth no more inspire thee?" Leave the dark regions of your mind, throw all away and fall down in idolatry before the sunset. I know my magic power to drive your griefs away. Few hearts so wildly weep on earth, yet few hearts ask that Heaven may be as like this earth as your heart does.

"Then let my winds caress thee;
Thy comrade let me be:
Since nought beside can bless thee,
Return and dwell with me."

With me, the moor, where in winter the hearts of voyagers beat with joy to feel the frost wind blow. What flower of the world is worth one flake of snow? The wind blows.

"Yes—I could swear that glorious wind
Has swept the world aside,
Has dashed its memory from thy mind
Like foam-bells from the tide."

In the wind a spirit flies, the essence of the tempests roaring, a universal influence.

And to this earth, of moor, of sunset and of wind, Emily cries: Heaven can never give my spirit rest. The children of heaven know nought akin to mortal despair, nor what tenant haunts the mortal body, nor what gloomy guest dwells in the mortal heart. Oh, earth! on your kindly breast let me be laid, and if I waken, let me share with you a "mutual immortality."

When I am dead, bury me on the hill. Let ling and heather be my grave flowers and the moor wind stir the moor grass upon my tomb, may my spirit wander with the cloud above me, my body rot to mould, may I become the earth and sky for Heaven is not my place. Why? Because this moor is my home? No—because no promised Heaven could all or half fulfil the wild desires of my heart, no hell subdue my quenchless will. Give me rest, rest and escape from Heaven and hell and the world.

Poor soul! She seeks rest in "the earth that wakes *one* human heart to feeling," the earth that centres "both the worlds of Heaven and Hell".

> "In the earth—the earth—thou shalt be laid,
>   A grey stone standing over thee;
> Black mould beneath thee spread
>   And black mould to cover thee.
>
> "Well—there is rest there,
>   So fast come thy prophecy;
> The time when my sunny hair
>   Shall with grass roots entwinèd be."

But the fierce fight is not over yet. In the Dark Tower is neither peace nor rest. In vain shall Childe Roland pray.

> "Oh, for the time when I shall sleep
>   Without identity,
> And never care how rain may steep,
>   Or snow may cover me!"

He shall drink of the "divinest anguish" compared to which the sufferings of his medium years are as nothing, he shall know again the "darling pain" that wounded

183

and seared his childhood, the "desire for nothing known" in his "maturer years," for the white spirit, the great white whale, whiteness, the Fair Lover.

When will men know that the Fair Lover carries a sword? They have been told. They do not hear. He comes not to take us to the land of the Lotus Eaters, nor to Lethe nor the quiet fields of some pastoral heaven. He comes to kill men for their souls. There is Hell, there is Eden, there is Heaven. Those that go to Heaven die upon the flaming sword. The Dark Hero in us fights to the bitter end the Spirit that he seeks.

Only God's innocents, of whom some few are born, never feel God's sword. They neither feel nor fear it.

Emily Jane Brontë was not one of these.

XXVI

AUNT BRANWELL'S SAVINGS ARE IN
DANGER A SECOND TIME

"Courage, boys! courage!"
Emily to "exiled and harassed Anne"

ON the surface everything went well in 1841.
Family life was made up of many persons,
and a web is woven that covers very much
of personalities and prophets; family life, that has a
texture of family peace, can cover even dominions and
angels.

Between the "torments and madness, tears and sin" of
July 17th, the rest from "weeks of wild delirium past,
Weeks of fevered pain," that comes on September 1st,
Charlotte arrived home from her new situation at Mr.
White's for a holiday. She had tried again to be a
governess. She went in February to Mr. White's at
Upperwood House, Rawdon near Bradford. She had
two children of six and eight under her, "nor such little
devils incarnate as the Sidgwicks." She found it hard
to "repel the rude familiarity of children"; and called
nursing a fat baby, during the spring cleaning, a bene-
ficial exertion. Glad am I that Charlotte never tutored
me!

Charlotte, I fear, was also become a snob. She, grand-
daughter of Peasant Prunty, was convinced that "Mr.

White's extraction is very low." Well could she believe that Mrs. White was only an exciseman's daughter. In truth the Whites were very kind to her, asked her father to be their guest, and were ever ready to receive her friends, but she would not bend nor melt. Frozen stiff and bored, she kept apart from them from beginning to end.

Before these holidays which are to have such significance Charlotte wrote the following letter to Emily, which shows that she kept her pulse on family affairs:

"Dear E-J.,—I received your last letter with delight as usual. I must write a line to thank you for it and the inclosure, which, however, is too bad—you ought not to have sent me those packets. I had a letter from Anne yesterday; she says she is well. I hope she speaks absolute truth. I had written to her and Branwell a few days before. I have not heard from Branwell yet. It is to be hoped that his removal to another [railway] station [Luddenfoot] will turn out for the best. As you say, it *looks* like getting on at any rate."

Branwell evidently was a cause of worry to Charlotte and Emily already. The rest of the letter concerns a holiday she had asked for. "I stuck to my point in a very exemplary and remarkable manner," and winds up with a discussion of Mary Taylor's affairs.

On May 9th she wrote to that Henry Nussey, Ellen's brother, who had once proposed to her and with whom she corresponded occasionally. In it she referred to her life at home.

"My home is humble and unattractive to strangers,

186

but to me it contains what I shall find nowhere else in the world—the profound, the intense affection which brothers and sisters feel for each other when their minds are cast in the same mould, their ideas drawn from the same source—when they have clung to each other from childhood, and when disputes have never sprung up to divide them."

A strange mould it must have been that formed both Emily's and Charlotte's mind!

"Emily is the only one left at home, where her usefulness and willingness make her indispensable." Emily's indispensability was not always called that name by Charlotte. Within a short time Charlotte was going to attack it and make it very dispensable, she was going to stick in "a very exemplary and remarkable manner," to a point, a scheme that soon began to brew in her mind, and Emily's hard-earned willingness would be set at naught.

In order to make all matters clear, I must revert to the affairs of Charlotte's dear friends, Mary and Martha Taylor. These girls had lost their father, the home was broken up and they had to turn out and ultimately earn their living. About this time, Charlotte nearly took up some job in Ireland; afterwards she offered the "Irish concern" to Mary Taylor. But Mary refused it for family reasons. The Taylors' project was to go to New Zealand. Try France for a year, suggested Charlotte. Betwixt June and August Mary visited Brussels, where Martha, it seems, enjoyed "great advantage."

In July Charlotte went home for three weeks and

187

revived in that holiday a plan for borrowing money from Aunt Branwell to set up a school along with Emily and Anne.

Emily seems to have received the scheme with enthusiasm. Anne hoped it would come off. She was at the Robinsons now, the Robinsons who were to be made protagonists in a drama of ghosts.

How Charlotte could ever long for a school of "little devils incarnate," or Emily glow over the notion of a "pleasant and flourishing seminary," I cannot imagine.

Apparently while Emily was writing "we . . . shall be all merrily seated in our own sitting-room in some pleasant and flourishing seminary. . . . It will be a fine, warm summer evening, very different from this bleak look-out," for Anne's perusal, and wondering aloud for Anne, if "we shall still be dragging on in our present condition," she was suffering wild delirium and pain.

Perhaps she was momentarily excited at the prospect of change, or rest from brewing and baking, from shirt-making and sweeping. Anne and Charlotte were not home to see her suffer any reaction. It is easy to hide feelings under writing.

Charlotte, of course, engineered the new undertaking, and thus she set about doing so.

"There is a project hatching in this house, which both Emily and I anxiously wished to discuss with you," she wrote to Ellen Nussey on July 19th—"To come to the point, papa and aunt talk, by fits and starts, of our—*id est*, Emily, Anne, and myself—commencing a school. I have often, you know, said how much I wished such a

188

thing; but I never could conceive where the capital was to come from for making such a speculation." Now, Aunt Branwell had been *tried* some time before and had wisely refused to part with the shekels. "I always considered she [Aunt] was the last person who would offer a loan for the purpose in question." But on this occasion, Aunt intimated that perhaps she might offer a loan if the scheme showed signs of maturing. Charlotte settled in her mind on borrowing £150 from her. "As to getting into debt, that is a thing we could none of us reconcile our minds to for a moment." Presumably the "we" included poor Miss Branwell who had as good as lost her money already, with that "intimation."

In August Charlotte wrote from Upperwood House (Mrs. White's): "No further steps have been taken about the project I mentioned to you . . . but Emily, and Anne, and I keep it in view. It is our polar star, and we look to it under all circumstances of despondency."

Soon after this it was proposed that Charlotte should take on Dewsbury Moor, Miss Wooler's school, but that lady's reply to Charlotte's letter of acceptance delayed to arrive. In that case Aunt's money would not have been needed as Miss Wooler was prepared to lend the furniture, but Charlotte had in the meantime got a "strong wish for wings"; in a word, she wanted to go to Brussels to the Taylors to see cathedrals and pictures. It would assist the school scheme to learn French, Brussels was cheaper than Paris, and so Aunt's kind offer of £100 ought to be laid out in acquiring the French language,

189

Italian and a "dash of German" at Brussels. "These are advantages which would turn to vast account . . . and, if Emily could share them with me, only for a single half-year. . . ." Aunt was subsequently flattered into acquiescence. Then in November Charlotte wrote to Ellen Nussey a statement of affairs. Dewsbury Moor was relinquished, but in spite of that, and I suppose the renewed necessity of capital for the school itself, the Brussels scheme was stuck to. "I wished for one, at least, of my sisters to share the advantage with me. I fixed on Emily. She deserved the reward, I knew."

On November 7th she wrote to Emily. "Belgium is a long way off and people are everywhere hard to spur up to the proper speed. (Aunt presumably!) Grieve not over Dewsbury Moor. *You were cut out there to all intents and purposes, so in fact was Anne;* Miss Wooler would hear of neither for the first half-year." [1] Charlotte had evidently seen that "polar star" of Emily's and Anne's set with the greatest complacency, and had told them nothing of its decline until it suited her purpose.

"Before our half-year in Brussels is completed," Charlotte continued, "you and I will have to seek employment abroad. *It is not my intention to retrace my steps home till twelve months,* if all continues well—"

Things hung fire until Christmas Eve then Charlotte went home to clinch the matter of actual destination, Lille or Brussels, to get Aunt's money for a purpose that was not on the original programme. She ap-

---

[1] The italics here and below are mine.

190

parently said nothing about that extra six months.

One has to forgive Charlotte a certain amount of duplicity. She certainly played Aunt Branwell as a skilful angler plays a trout, but the idea of Brussels had gone to her head, and an idea once fixed in Charlotte's head could not easily be routed. It is easy to understand what dreams the very notion of foreign travel wakened in the heart of Charlotte, the proud ambitious little creature cooped up in the ambiguous isolation of a governess.

"Grieve not over Dewsbury Moor!" If a vision of Eldorado had not come, of the Eldorado of pictures and cathedrals and learning, Dewsbury Moor would have hardly been dismissed so gaily from Charlotte's mind— Dewsbury Moor that nearly killed Anne once according to Charlotte—the school that heretofore had been a living tomb to Emily.

Why did Charlotte want Emily to go to Brussels? How reconcile the phrases "Emily deserved the reward," and "the experiment was tried of sending her to school again"?

Men are self-deceivers ever.

How reconcile Emily's lines written for Anne, which I have already quoted, and her words addressed to Heaven, in the midst of hearing Charlotte's projects for school keeping:—

> "Sweet land of light! thy children fair
> Know nought akin to our despair.
>
> .   .   .   .   .
>
> "At least we would not bring them down
> With us to weep, with us to groan."

191

When Emily turned deceiver, she could do the job consciously and well. Had she not earlier in the year defined her attitude toward life and prayed her prayer, prayed that she might have liberty for her inner life and courage to endure the world?

"Riches I hold in light esteem,
  And Love I laugh to scorn;
And lust of fame was but a dream,
  That vanished with the morn:

"And if I pray, the only prayer
  That moves my lips for me
Is, 'Leave the heart that now I bear,
  And give me liberty!'

"Yes, as my swift days near their goal,
  'Tis all that I implore;—
In life and death a chainless soul,
  And courage to endure."

Thus spoke she in the guise of an Old Stoic, though you may take it that the first verse is a renunciation rather than a fact, and that the rest is but a paraphrase of those famous flippant lines:—

"I care for nobody, no, not I!
And nobody cares for me!"

The whole thing amounts to a definition of Childe Roland's attitude toward the heaven and earth of his fellow men.

Emily did not chop and change. Deep down she

wanted Riches and Fame, deeper down Love, and at bottom longed to, but could not, make the great surrender. Pity she was not provided with a war into which she might have gone and perished quickly while still the spirit of the thing cried, "For God and the King! St. George for Merry England!"

That great surrender is something more than death, but it is only saints and young heroes who perish joyously on the sword of God. It is not a mere dying, dying won't do it. I'll tell you this, men that come home from a long war, come home sad. When they find they are not dead, and no longer heroes they think God, even if by word they don't believe in God, they think He has refused them, turned them down.

Wars do not concern us here. That is only a hint how to find Emily, the Dark Hero, in you and me.

"Blow, bugles blow! They brought us for our dearth
Holiness, lacked so long, and Love, and Pain.
Honour has come back, as a king, to earth."

So sang Rupert Brooke of death and the soldier, death that "leaves a white unbroken glory" and "a shining peace, under the night."

What of us who are not dead, and those who must die in their own battles on a lonely battlefield?

XXVII

THE LAND OF PROMISE

" . . . A fire was kindled in my very heart, which I could not quench. I so longed to increase my attainments—to become something better than I am."
Charlotte Brontë to Ellen Nussey about Brussels

"Once more she seemed sinking, but this time she rallied through the mere force of resolution: with inward remorse and shame she looked back on her former failure, and resolved to conquer in this second ordeal."
Charlotte of Emily at Brussels

BY force of the nature of their employment, Christmas and midsummer were the only times when the Brontë girls all met in these years.

Charlotte left the Whites on Christmas Eve, 1841, and came home to Emily and Mr. Weightman and Anne who was on holiday from the Robinsons. Mr. Weightman entertained himself that Christmas-tide by making eyes at Anne, but the poor fellow's last illness was already upon him.

Charlotte was going abroad for certain and to that end the house was engaged once more in making substantial underwear. Aunt had promised Emily and Charlotte fifty pounds apiece to pay their way for six

194

months; afterwards—Charlotte meant to take care of the afterwards.

It was not until nearly the last minute that the actual destination of the two young women was decided upon. How could it be in the Brontë family? Lille, Brussels —Brussels, Lille; at last it was determined that they should go to the Pensionnat Héger (which has become Haygar forever on Yorkshire tongues) in Brussels, and in February, 1842, Old Brontë dug himself out of the Parsonage and took his two pale-faced daughters, aged twenty-five and twenty-three, to school there, to sleep and eat and learn with children on an average ten years younger. Charlotte, according to French ideas and doubtless Belgian, had already entered upon the vocation of Old Maid. Emily, gaunt, and sallow and masculine, must have seemed to the cheerful, fat daughters of Brussels a veritable amphibian out of water.

But still, for Charlotte, at least, Brussels under any conditions was the Land of Promise.

The three queer companions spent a night on the way in London at the Chapter Coffee House, a brown old hostel in the shadow of Saint Paul's. They set sail from mid Thames and crossed to Ostend presumably. Charlotte was no sailor. Papa coached with them to Brussels and left them at the great old house of Madame Héger in the Rue d'Isabelle, without detaining himself beyond one night in Brussels City.

Emily and Charlotte were admitted into the school by a portress in a smart cap, who though a spy of Madame Héger according to *Villette,* was not above taking a sovereign on occasion from one of the young scholar's admirers.

They found themselves in a school of near one hundred girls, of whom about twenty were boarders, a first-class school for daughters of the rich, no genteel seminary run by narrow-minded old maids. Good teaching, good food, good quarters were provided for the scholars, some of whom were of the best Belgian families.

This old house with its great bare parqueted rooms and French windows, its orchard-garden at the back needs not my hand to describe it. It exists for ever in *Villette*, Madame Héger and Monsieur Héger, the "insane tom-cat," the "little black being," the "delirious hyena" of Charlotte's first letters, this pair of extraordinary persons, their satellites, their surroundings, down to the minutest details of white beds, toilettes, "malle fermant à clef," the food, the orchard-garden surrounded by a high wall, the "allée défendue" overlooked by one window of the male Academy adjoining the garden—that window of the Athénée which played such an important part in Charlotte's imagination; there, in Brussels at the Pensionnat Héger, these things existed in real life, almost as real as in *Villette*.

The young ladies of the establishment were always well, though simply, dressed. On fête days they blossomed out in white book-muslin, organdy and wide ribbon sashes, looking like coryphées in classical ballet, with satin brodequins, smoothed hair, and flowers, lumpish Taglionis, but still young and fresh and jolly.

Do you see Emily in her straight hanging silk gown of some dreary hue with leg-o'-mutton sleeves, and Charlotte, a little grey ghost making merry with these nymphs? By way of religion there were candles, incense and silver hearts and a million feminine lies.

Emily must have felt dark and heroic indeed among the pantomime peris of Charlotte's paradise.

Had she been younger, and the daughter of a millionaire, and on her own, Emily, with very small doubt, saw herself in that state making a brilliant mark on the annals of the Academy. But being a stoic, she wore ridiculous sleeves and fought with M. Héger.

Alas, from the scant material at hand, it is difficult to draw a complete picture of Emily's life in Brussels. At present I can find only two poems of hers with the date 1842 after them. Both are love poems of sorts and belong to the guilt cycle. Taken by themselves they mean nothing in particular. In *Villette* Emily does not figure. That is the history of Charlotte's second residence in Brussels, rather than of the first, though of course this first year is woven into the book to form its texture. As a "novel" *Villette* is the best of all the Brontë works, as a three-decker novel full of human experience in middle-earth. Charlotte did not allow herself in these days to hear the cock crow. She was human, and that warning to be away from men was not for her. It was Emily who "went away," whose place was not here among men and women and pensionnats, earthly love, earthly sorrow and joy.

In Charlotte's world, however, she managed to stay

or had to stay nine months. I do not suppose she had a farthing to bless herself with, to enable her to escape in a bodily sense even if she wished to. Whatever she suffered under the wardership of Charlotte, this one grace fate allowed her. She came into conflict with a first-class masculine mind. Charlotte said of Emily that she and M. Héger did not "draw well together"; but M. Héger said of Emily, "She should have been a man— a great navigator. Her powerful reason would have deduced new spheres of discovery from the knowledge of the old; and her strong, imperious will would never have been daunted by opposition or difficulty; never have given way but with life."

He soon saw that Charlotte and Emily had best be taught by superior methods suited to their minds, taught to think straight, to analyze and synthesize. He read them Hugo, Guizot, Bossuet, according to Mrs. Gaskell whose inaccuracy is feminine in the extreme. Emily was provided with the best music master in Belgium for the piano. She also took German lessons and learned drawing. Very presently she read the tales of Hoffmann in the original, what other German works I do not know. She gave a drawing, I have heard, to a Mademoiselle de Bassompière, a pupil in the school— do not start at the familiarity of the name. This drawing of one of the great trees in the school garden is said to be still in the possession of the family.

Charlotte says Emily worked like a horse, and made rapid progress in spite of the great difficulties she had

198

to contend with. M. Héger gave the pair of them sundry private lessons.

The six months for which Aunt had payed came to an end, and either by suggestion or coincidence, it came to pass, even as Charlotte had more or less designed from the start, that she and Emily remained on in Brussels. I do not take much stock of her letter on the subject. Suffice it to say that it suited Madame to have her teach English in return for continued instruction and board and lodging, and that Emily on her part was put to instruct some of the smaller musicians of the school in scales and five-finger exercises.

Two perfectly divergent traditions survive of Emily's behaviour and aspect at school. According to Mrs. Gaskell, M. Héger found her egotistical and selfish, unconsciously tyrannical over Charlotte and obtuse to other people's reasoning. According to Mary Taylor she was almost perfectly silent when "asked out" by friends. Letitia Wheelwright, an English scholar and part-boarder, found her too unamiable to entertain and said both she and Charlotte were friendless and lonely.

On the other hand I have heard that Emily was liked and admired at school, and that when she left the school Madame gave her a book, a present of esteem. M. Héger, like Mr. Brontë, considered Emily the greater genius.

Charlotte drew for publication an extreme picture of her unhappiness at Brussels.

All that really signifies at the moment is that for the first time Emily met with genuine and valuable

199

appreciation of her powers and heard discourse of books and other matters from a man of intellect and character.

"When you have thrown the reins on the neck of your imagination, do not pull her up to reason."

The man who spoke thus must have drawn some feelings of appreciation, recognition and fellowship from Emily however badly he and she got on together in a general way.

Of her attitude toward Catholics, her clinging to Charlotte, her homesickness, Mrs. Gaskell, who thought that Emily in general deserved being disliked, and Charlotte, whose testimony in the dock, so to speak is not above suspicion, have a fair amount to say.

You may if you like imagine Emily leaning upon little Charlotte, tirading against Jesuitry and Popish Idolatry, bewailing the Parsonage and the moors in tragic tones.

Or you may imagine her discovering a world of cathedrals and pictures, spurred by these realities of art to learn to read the masters of French and German literature, to learn to draw for herself, not copies of mezzotints, but the beautiful old trees in the garden, to learn to interpret the masters of music upon the piano.

Had she no sense of kinship with the German Romantics whom she here encountered? Did the dark candle-lit interior of the cathedral rouse no thought in her?

Whatever she got from Brussels lay fallow for one

year, and then, from 1844 to 1846 Emily wrote the best things of her life. Strength and certainty are added to power. Emily, the man of genius, has words and thought at her complete command.

I will not say she did not hate the Belgians and the Pensionnat and her situation there. I will not say she did not shake the dust of Brussels from her feet with determination never again to soil herself therewith. I will not even say she was not unhappy, a woman turned twenty-four in a smart girls' school.

Charlotte told the world that she behaved, to begin with, as she did at Dewsbury Moor, but for shame conquered herself at great cost and almost died of the victory.

Make of it all what you can. Remember that there she met Hoffmann and Hugo in print, and Hoffmann, at least, accompanied her in her life thereafter. Stranger friendships have been made in stranger places than this between Childe Roland and the Romantic German in a Catholic School for fashionable foreign misses.

To end this chapter I quote here in full a poem begun at Brussels on October 23rd before Emily knew she was going to leave, and finished several months later when she was at home alone again. The poor Stoic is in a very bad way, as self-made stoics are apt to be. Behold his Self-Interrogation. This poem belongs to the Guilt cycle. I warn you not to surmise that Emily performed some awful deed at Brussels. It is quite clear which lines of the poem belong to Brussels and very few they are. But there is an air of Hope defeated again,

201

of ambition again crushed down, as if she had dared to try and escape her fate at Brussels.

"SELF-INTERROGATION"

" 'The evening passes fast away,
    'Tis almost time to rest;
What thoughts has left the vanished day?
    What feelings in thy breast?

" 'The vanished day? It leaves a sense
    Of labour hardly done;
Of little gained with vast expense—
    A sense of grief alone!

" 'Time stands before the door of Death,
    Upbraiding bitterly;
And Conscience, with exhaustless breath,
    Pours black reproach on me:

" 'And though I've said that Conscience lies,
    And Time should Fate condemn;
Still, sad Repentance clouds my eyes,
    And makes me yield to them!'

" 'Then art thou glad to seek repose?
    Art glad to leave the sea,
And anchor all thy weary woes
    In calm Eternity?

" 'Nothing regrets to see thee go—
    Not one voice sobs "Farewell";
And where thy heart has suffered so,
    Canst thou desire to dwell?'

" 'Alas! the countless links are strong
    That bind us to our clay;
The loving spirit lingers long,   .
    And would not pass away!

" 'And rest is sweet, when laurelled fame
    Will crown the soldier's crest;
But a brave heart, with a *tarnished* name,
    Would rather fight than rest.'

" 'Well, thou hast fought for many a year,
    Hast fought thy whole life through,
Hast humbled Falsehood, trampled Fear;
    What is there left to do?'

" ' 'Tis true, this arm has hotly striven,
    Has dared what few would dare;
Much have I done, and freely given,
    But little learnt to bear!'

" 'Look on the grave where thou must sleep,
    Thy last, and strongest foe;
It is endurance not to weep
    If that repose seem woe.

" 'The long war closing in defeat—
    Defeat serenely borne,—
Thy midnight rest may still be sweet,
    And break in glorious morn!' "

XXVIII

DEATH THE DESPOT

"Now, no more a cheerful ranger,
Following pathways known of yore,
Sad he stood, a wild-eyed stranger,
On his own unbounded moor?"
                    Emily Jane Brontë

AUNT BRANWELL died.

Her funeral knell rang Charlotte and Emily home from Brussels. Its tones were three times heard this October. William Weightman preceded Aunt to the grave by a few days, and in Brussels Martha Taylor left this life to Charlotte's sorrow in the same month.

"Aunt, Martha Taylor, and Mr. Weightman are now all gone; how dreary and void everything seems," she wrote. Did Emily, among her many dirges, write one for any of these three?

Charlotte and Emily arrived home too late to see anything of Miss Branwell, but her Will, dated 1833. Under that Will, Charlotte and Emily and Anne found themselves each legatees, with a female cousin, as to one-fourth of somewhere between 1,000 and 1,500 pounds. Emily Jane received as her personal mementoes, a workbox with a China top and an ivory fan. Branwell was remembered only to the extent of a Japan dressing-box, Aunt doubtless supposing that he would be more able to support himself than the girls.

Not long after Aunt's demise, Ellen Nussey came to stay, and Charlotte's spirits quite revived. By January she was as gay as could be. M. Héger had written to Mr. Brontë (the given date of his letter, October 5th, must be incorrect) offering to create situations for one or both of his late pupils.

An "irresistible impulse" caused Charlotte to accept his invitation "against her conscience." She returned in a very short while to the Pensionnat as English teacher at £16 a year, all found, but washing five francs a month. She was her own mistress to the extent of about the same amount of private income.

Well, it is not now considered a disgrace for a young woman to fall in love before she is "asked" to have private passions and real feelings about men. Love blows where it wills. It was not Charlotte's fault that M. Héger was married. We should rejoice at this sad state of affairs, for otherwise where would *Jane Eyre* and *Villette* be now, but in the region of the unborn? Knowing how Charlotte could not leave go of any desire that possessed her, imagine the torture that she endured in proximity to M. Héger. She simply forced herself to walk in the straight and narrow way.

Turn to *Villette* if you want to know what Charlotte came to feel for M. Héger, if you want to know what "real confession" she made to the old priest in Brussels Cathedral, which confession she described to Emily as an "odd whim" to "yield a moment's interest," "a freak."

In so far as she was aware, Charlotte behaved, I am certain, with heroic propriety under these circumstances; but though she knew her hopeless case, she could not apparently leave Brussels. Mary Taylor, it appears, in the end assisted her to rescue herself. What the parting with M. Héger cost her she thought she would never be able to forget—nor did she. She suffered much before she left Brussels.

During this year of agony to Charlotte, Emily stayed at home alone. Branwell was gone to the Robinsons, to suffer in due time by his own account as Charlotte suffered, but with less manly courage. Rumour has it that Papa Brontë was become somewhat too close a friend of the whisky bottle.

In May, Emily wrote a letter to "Miss Nussey" in which she said,

"Charlotte has never mentioned a word about coming home. If you would go over for half a year, perhaps you might be able to bring her back with you, otherwise she might vegetate there till the age of Methuseleh for mere lack of courage to face the voyage."

Not another word of Emily's normal life exists but one poem addressed presumably to Branwell, Anne and Charlotte calling them home to Gondal's "mists and moorlands drear" from "Ulah's gardens sweet."

But concerning the other side of the question, her inner life? Taking her poems of this year by themselves one might feel for a minute that Emily was bewitched by M. Héger or some inhabitant of Brussels even as

Charlotte was; but there has been too much of guilt and love and death before this date to warrant even an idle thought in this direction. In her loneliness, however, Emily found consolation. Her imagination discovered that it could make dreams to beguile her soul out of its misery and gloom. For a time she surrendered herself to Fancy, her fairy love, and in the realm of fantasy found rest and bliss.

> "How clear she shines! How quietly
> I lie beneath her silver light;
> While heaven and earth are whispering me,
> 'To-morrow, wake, but dream to-night.'
>
> "Yes, Fancy, come, my Fairy love!
> These throbbing temples softly kiss;
> And bend my lonely couch above,
> And bring me rest, and bring me bliss.
>
> "The world is going; dark world, adieu!
> Grim world, conceal thee till the day;
> The heart thou canst not all subdue
> Must still resist, if thou delay!"

There are strange narcotics sometimes within the power of man; a trancelike state can actually be created in the mind by sheer surrender of the will to imagination. People of a day-dreaming habit, especially if they possess visual imagination, can transport themselves absolutely out of this world into a realm of other reality. Once the trance is induced, the dream unfolds of itself about the body and soul of the dreamer. Soft breezes

207

blow which are actually felt by the senses. All the senses participate in the illusion. Emily had in full this ability to surrender herself to illusion.

People who have never dreamed thus in their waking hours cannot possibly realize the glorious rest from sorrow and from strife these visits to the world of Fancy bring. Imagine that you in the midst of toil and sorrow, instead of tossing throughout a sleepless night, walk out of this life into a city where the sun shines in a sky of Italian blue, and there encounter people it has never been your lot to meet on earth, people you can see about you as you see ordinary men, people who speak to you, not words put into their mouths by you, but their own words, born of thoughts *which are not yours*. There, in that city, many wonderful things happen. You are endowed with extraordinary powers. You astonish the citizens with a magnificent work of art, or build them a perfect bridge over yonder romantic chasm. In night-dreams these things happen, but madly. In day-dreams all is consecutive and real.

> "At such a time, in such a spot,
>   The world seems made of light;
> Our blissful hearts remember not,
>   How, surely follows night."

But this dream world would cease to charm if it were void of love. There fortunately in some garden or wood one meets the ideal being, sought in this world and never found, that Love which has none of the beauty of

tragedy, but all the beauty of bliss, a golden June of love.
The dreamer cries in worship:—

> "Then art thou not my golden June
>   All mist and tempest free?
> As shines earth's sun in summer noon
>   So heaven's sun shines in thee."

> .   .   .   .   .

> "Oh, could it thus for ever be
>   That I might so adore;
> I'd ask for all eternity
> To make a paradise for me,
>   My love,—and nothing more."

Sometimes the dreamer indulges in luxurious tragedy.

> "I dreamt one sunny day like this,
>   In this peerless month of May,
> I saw her give th' unanswered kiss
>   As his spirit passed away.

> "Those young eyes that so sweetly shine
>   Then looked their last adieu,
> And pale death changed that cheek divine
>   To his unchanging hue."

Fancy does not always prove to be a very excellent
poet. Were all her creations as mawkish as these, her
narcotic would soon cloy. But she has other dreams,
more sombre, with a thrill of phantoms and death and
tragedy. Although Emily Brontë cried:—

> "And this shall be my dream to-night;
>   I'll think the heaven of glorious spheres
> Is rolling on its course of light
>   In endless bliss, through endless years;

"I'll think, there's not one world above,
  Far as these straining eyes can see,
Where Wisdom ever laughed at Love,
  Or Virtue crouched to Infamy;

"Where, writhing 'neath the strokes of Fate,
  The mangled wretch was forced to smile;
To match his patience 'gainst her hate,
  His heart rebellious all the while;

"Where Pleasure still will lead to wrong,
  And helpless Reason warn in vain;
And Truth is weak, and Treachery strong;
  And Joy the surest path to Pain;

"And Peace, the lethargy of Grief;
  And Hope, a phantom of the soul;
And Life, a labour, void and brief;
  And Death, the despot of the whole!"

yet her finest day-dreams of this time had a mournful
tone, and many a time she dreamed of ghosts and heroic
death and tragic love. She loved the tragic muse for
all her praise of June.

"How do I love to hear the flow
  Of Aspin's water, murmuring low;
  And hours long listen to the breeze
  That sighs in Beckden's waving trees!

"To-night there is no wind to wake
  One ripple on the lovely lake;
  To-night the clouds, subdued and grey,
  Starlight and moonlight shut away."

In that "calm and still and almost drear" solitude, she saw ghosts, the ghost of one who died for love, and of another for whom that first "spirit, unforgiven" wandered "unsheltered, shut from Heaven,—An outcast for eternity."

Another day she dreamed of battle, of the fall of her dream-city Zalona, where "emerald flags stream broad and gay," green flags of Hope, Hope the phantom of her soul. Hope lost the battle. Alas! the grim reality of her earthly sorrow stole in upon her dreams. Fancy had already begun to lose its influence upon her soul. Like other narcotics, in time its power waned. At the end of this year she dreamed a hero's death and, in the moment of his dying, wrote these lines in which echoes the despair of her own heart:—

"Look up and see
The twilight fading from the skies:
That last dim beam that sets for thee,
Roderic, for thee shall never rise!"

Even though she tried to think that there was no world where Death ruled in omnipotence, Fancy proved in the end a frail comforter and was unable to disguise from her the truth she felt in her own heart, that "Hope was but a timid friend," and "Death, the despot of the whole!"

The game is nearly up as regards Emily's humanity. The Dark Hero in her heart is in the ascendent. She is still able to escape him in dreams for a while. Very soon there will be no more visits to the world of fancy

211

or to the real world for Childe Roland. Then his only freedom from the Dark Tower will be upon the moor, and there he will become finally possessed by that spirit who has dominated his life since youth, who has driven him from the world to this sombre place, and who will finally drive him down to seek oblivion in the grave.

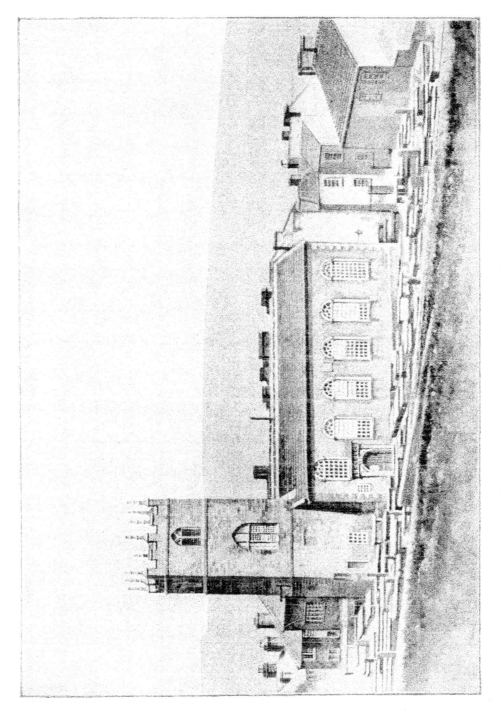

HAWORTH CHURCH AND GRAVEYARD

This was practically the view from the Parsonage windows in the Brontës' time

Reproduced by permission of Mr. John Grant from "Lives of the Brontës"

XXIX

THE HIDDEN GHOST

"And I am rough and rude, yet not more rough to see
Than is the hidden ghost that has its home in me."
                                    Emily Jane Brontë

IN January, 1844, Charlotte came home to Haworth, and at once began to agitate a mad scheme for turning the Parsonage into a school for young ladies. Aunt's legacy was to be spent in building on an extra room or two, and in setting the business on its feet.

The thing went so far that a circular advertising for pupils was actually printed, but fortunately for all concerned, no pupil ever applied for admission. Charlotte kept up some sort of belief in her scheme for a whole year.

She found Haworth "a lonely, quiet spot, buried away from the world," after Brussels. The quiet of this year was varied with few incidents. Charlotte paid a visit to Ellen Nussey, Ellen Nussey sent Emily a present of flower seeds, the Sicilian pea and crimson corn-flower, for which she was much obliged, and asked if they "should be sown in warm and sheltered situations?" The cat died. Emily was sorry. Ellen Nussey paid a visit to Haworth. Emily and Charlotte made many shirts. Mr.

Weightman's successor, Mr. Smith, the curate, showed marked attention to Miss Nussey. Emily and Charlotte walked out a great deal together on the moors. All very small matters.

Anne and Branwell came home in June from the Robinsons for a holiday. Mr. Smith was replaced by Mr. Grant, temporarily, until Mr. Arthur Bell Nicholls arrived to be curate at Haworth for many a year. The Brontës took his second name when they turned author. The "Currer" that Charlotte put before the "Bell," she borrowed from an old and well-known family in the neighbourhood. That is by the way. These three curates figure, not too brilliantly, in *Shirley*; Nicholls, Charlotte's "future" comes out the best of the three. In real life she called him "narrow-minded Mr. Nicholls" a "highly uninteresting, narrow, and unattractive specimen of the coarser sex."

Branwell "was more than ordinarily troublesome and annoying" that autumn and led old Brontë "a wretched life." How his behaviour reconciled itself with the duties of tutor to Mr. Robinson's children, I do not know.

Not a word more can be squeezed out of Charlotte's letters to enliven 1844.

Perhaps this was the year in which Emily was bitten by the mad dog. It seems to have happened in the days of Keeper, Emily's second bull-dog, and after Aunt's death. Charlotte not only told Mrs. Gaskell about it, but described the incident in *Shirley*. The story may as well be told again, and in Charlotte's words. To make a straight tale of it, I will quote from *Shirley* such sentences as are necessary, without dots and dashes to show what I have left out.

"A dog," says Shirley [Emily] to Mr. Moore, who for the moment is in Charlotte's place; "a dog came running up the lane. The poor creature ran with her head down, her tongue hanging out; she looked as if bruised and beaten all over. When I attempted to pat her head, she turned and snatched at my arm. She bit it so to draw blood. Mr. Wynne's keeper came up, carrying a gun. He said, 'She is raging mad.'

" 'And you told no one, sought no help?'

" 'Yes: I walked straight into the laundry, took an Italian iron from the fire, and applied the light scarlet glowing tip to my arm: I bored it well in: it cauterised the little wound.'

" 'I daresay you never once groaned.'

" 'I am sure I don't know. I was very miserable. Not firm or tranquil at all, I think.'

" 'You disdain sympathy.'

" 'Do I?'

" 'With your powerful mind, you must feel independent of help, of device, of society.'

" 'So be it—since it pleases you.'

" 'If it is not so, how is it, then?'

" 'I don't know.'

" 'You do know, but you won't speak: all must be locked up in yourself.'

" 'Because it is not worth sharing.'

" 'Because nobody can give the high price you require

215

for your confidence. Nobody has the honour, the intellect, the power you demand in your adviser. Of course you must live alone.'

" 'I *can* live alone, if need be. But the question is not how to live—but how to die alone. That strikes me in a more grisly light.' "

This gruesome episode ends up with instructions how Shirley wished to be put out of her misery if she dedeveloped hydrophobia. She says to her companion.

" 'If I give trouble, with your own hand, administer to me a strong narcotic: such a sure dose of laudanum as shall leave no mistake.' " She will not have the doctors in to smother her out of life, which apparently was the local way of finishing off persons with hydrophobia. That seems to have been all she feared and that fear the sole reason for the disclosure of the accident. Shirley, at least, gained her point without yielding an inch of her soul to Mr. Moore.

Did Charlotte also promise Emily the same favour? I feel certain that she did, and after the same fruitless attempt to break down her reserve.

There was another famous dog-episode in Emily's life, the affair with Keeper. He, poor dog, liked to lie on beds, to Tabby's disgust. She, by now was back at the Parsonage. Emily promised to punish him if he was caught at it again. She had been warned that he would turn ferocious if he were beaten. Nevertheless, the next time he was found on his favourite lounge, Emily, white of face and with tight pressed lips, dragged him downstairs into a corner of the hall and punched him in the muzzle till his eyes swelled up. After this harsh treatment she bathed the wretched creature and soothed his pain herself. He, dog-like, worshipped her ever after and moped for her when she was no more.

The picture of poor Emily battering poor Keeper, and their mutual looking into one another's eyes afterwards, is indeed sad. As they crouched in his lair together, she feeling for his loneliness and he miserably repentant I doubt who was the wretcheder.

"Meantime," as Charlotte wrote in March, 1845, "life wears away." She will soon be thirty, and nothing yet done. Nothing has come yet of Roe Head School and Brussels Pensionnat so hardly won. Haworth was once a pleasant place to Charlotte. "It is not so now." Ellen Nussey's letters and the French newspapers "are the only messengers" from the outer world.

The blessed French newspapers circulate from hand to hand, and wind up with Mr. T. Dixon, care of Mr. J. of Sheffield. Who sent these reminders of too dear a time I cannot tell. Charlotte no longer writes to M. Héger. Gossip has given ugly enough reasons for that cessation of correspondence. Emily reads the French papers too during their three days' pause in their peregrinations at Haworth.

In June, 1845, Anne left the Robinsons for ever and Branwell accompanied her for a week's holiday; the atmosphere was ominous; clouds were gathering on the Brontë horizon. In the lull before the storm, Charlotte payed a visit to Hathersage in Derbyshire to stay with Henry Nussey and his wife, the wife that Charlotte might have been. Ellen was a fellow guest. It was the memory of this visit that Charlotte used in *Jane Eyre*. How well I know the spot! There the moors fall into a glorious valley, a lovely green valley of river and trees. The river winds down between the ramp of hills to the south past Hassop where the real Eyre [1] family came from, and on past Chatsworth. There is Haddon Hall within a drive and Peveril Castle within another. Little John is traditionally buried in Hathersage Churchyard. This romantic vale is called the Hope Valley, and indeed the valley of Hope it seems among the high frowning mountains that surround it.

This visit marks the end of many things for the Brontës and the beginning of the end of all.

There is to be no more peace at Haworth, but degradation and high achievement, fame, disappointment and death.

[1] Whose name alone was borrowed by Charlotte. The Eyres were to Hassop what the Manners were to Bakewell.

XXX

RUSTLING WINGS. THE BEGINNING OF
THE END

"Burn then, little lamp; glimmer straight and clear—
Hush! a rustling wing stirs, methinks, the air:
He for whom I wait thus ever comes to me;
Strange Power! I trust thy might; trust thou my constancy."
Emily Jane Brontë

HOW shall one die alone? "Drear the course that has been run, And dim the hearts that slowly die." Without the aid of some comforter, the most despairing soul would not have courage, even to commit suicide. Emily had created herself a comforter of sorts out of Fancy, but Fancy was beginning to prove frail. What other comforter had she? Who was that other Comforter, that spirit whom she called forth from the night?

> "My spirit drank a mingled tone,
> Of seraph's song, and demon's moan."

She cried to this Voice to calm her resentful mood. While still she had not quite forgotten Fancy (welcoming that benignant power, though trusting not its phantom bliss), she put her faith in Liberty, who with

219

Fancy and herself held "undisputed sovereignty" over the "world within." Was Liberty the name of the seraph-demon who came to her "in Heaven's glorious sun, And in the glare of Hell"? Was it Liberty who comforted her in face of that sin for which she might not be forgiven? Was Liberty the Radiant Angel for whom she cast the world away? Who was Liberty, and what was Liberty? Her slave, Fancy, whom as yet she ruled, whose fond creations, whose noonday dreams of the young lover June, whose Gondal dreams of knights and ladies still presented an illusion of reality—was this Liberty? Or was Liberty her King, that which she worshipped, her God of Visions?

Emily Brontë sometimes at this date confused that spirit of imagination, Fancy, her fairy love, her bright unharmful bringer of dreams, with the dark spirit that brought her visions. But this elf that was her sometime slave departed before that angel of night who had come to her in the earliest days of memory. Why did she still confuse these two? Because in the hour when the dark angel entered her heart, she had heard yet another voice, "so full of soul, so deeply sweet: I thought that Gabriel's self had come." Many a year had Gabriel's voice echoed in her heart when she was "all alone." Yet the day is long past since that sweet voice came to comfort her. It is not Gabriel now who comes to her at night across a waste of frozen snow, nor the wings of Gabriel that rustle through the air. This angel is a stranger Power, a Power of might, a "messenger of Hope," who "offers for short life, eternal liberty."

220

"He comes with western winds, with evening's wandering airs,
  With that clear dusk of heaven that brings the thickest stars.
  Winds take a pensive tone, and stars a tender fire,
  And visions rise, and change, that kill me with desire.

"Desire for nothing known in my maturer years
  When joy grew mad with awe, at counting future tears.
  When, if my spirit's sky was full of flashes warm,
  I knew not whence they came, from sun or thunder-storm."

Not yet does Emily perfectly realize whence come these desires, "from sun or thunder-storm." The Messenger of Eternal Liberty brings her "first, a hush of peace—a soundless calm."

"The struggle of distress, and fierce impatience ends;
  Mute music soothes my breast—unuttered harmony,
  That I could never dream, till Earth was lost to me.

"Then dawns the Invisible; the Unseen its truth reveals;
  My outward sense is gone, my inward essence feels:
  Its wings are almost free—its home, its harbour found,
  Measuring the gulf, it stoops—and dares the final bound.

"Oh! dreadful is the check—intense the agony—
  When the ear begins to hear, and the eye begins to see;
  When the pulse begins to throb, the brain to think again;
  The soul to feel the flesh, and the flesh to feel the chain.

"Yet I would lose no sting, would wish no torture less;
  The more that anguish racks, the earlier it will bless;
  And robed in fires of hell, or bright with heavenly shine,[1]
  If it but herald death, the vision is divine!"

Not thus have the saints entered heaven.

[1] The italics are mine.

At the supreme moment when the Messenger of Eternal Liberty has shown the Harmony of Heaven, the soul which "dares the final bound" feels the dreadful check. Liberty is again defeated, for there is no place for Liberty in the Hierarchy of Heaven. The defeated thing cries: May the anguish of defeat, whether it burns with the fire of Hellish desire, or shines as the unattainable glory of Heaven, destroy me utterly, that I may know oblivion!

Oblivion will not be gained yet awhile; the prisoner, the captive must dwell on in "constant darkness," must continue to suffer "this awful doom." It is useless to plead yet for release. The time has not yet come. It is useless to cry:

> "Oh, let me die—that power and will,
>   Their cruel strife may close."

>   .   .   .   .   .

> "O for the lid that cannot weep
>   The Breast that needs no breath
>   The tomb that brings eternal sleep
>   The traitor's Deliverer, Death!" [1]

The prisoner must continue many a day to track "the desert of despair." How *many spirits*, he cries, *driven through this false world* would give everything to win the *everlasting haven of death*. (But the devil still wanders up and down in the world and to and fro in it seeking repose.) Why does death strike the blessed

[1] These four last lines are the cancelled last lines of *The Philosopher*, for which were substituted the present last eight lines, of which the preceeding couplet forms part. I am indebted to C. W. Hatfield, Esq., for this information.

that do not desire this rest, and *yet shrinks appalled from his?* The groan of this poor wretch, his cry to oblivion, *has eclipsed the glory of the sky.*

The soul dies hard. Childe Roland, possessed of the devil, cries once or twice aloud, still in the name of life.

> "How beautiful the earth is still,
> To thee—how full of happiness!"

How can there still be happiness for Childe Roland? How can he still find glory in the spring and the delight of youth, when youth is dead and gone? Because he has hoped all his life and waited bliss. He early set aside "every phase of earthly joy," and "gazed o'er the sands the waves efface To the enduring seas." He cast the "anchor of desire Deep in unknown eternity"; "desire for nothing known in" his "maturer years"; "wild desires" which "no promised heaven" "could all, or half fulfil."

He never let his "spirit tire with looking for *what is to be!*" Unknown eternity he sets against what is to be. It is the unknown, the unutterable, the all he seems to crave. He wants more than what is to be. By that route the soul arrives at Complete Negation. Who sustains him in this quest? A glad comforter. Sustained by this comforter, his "spirit swells elate," "the more unjust seems present fate." *Strong, in the strength of this Angel,* Childe Roland can contemplate—rewarding destiny! O man of Destiny! desirer of the Unknown! O man of the All or None!

XXXI

"THE PHILOSOPHER"

"All Hope abandon, ye who enter here."
Inferno, Dante

FORSAKE the world and come away with me. As Virgil showed Dante the infernal shades I too will show you Hell. A hell of one man, a hell of only one man without the cheerful blaze of eternal flames without companionship of mutual torment as I and others know it full well to be.

Those who are afraid had best not come, for this is no tour of curiosity, but one by one each of you who choose shall come alone with me.

Turn your thoughts away from the green world, from the cities and sea and enter darkness. There stands the pride of Satan, a "space-sweeping soul." He cries aloud the cry of the damned.

"Oh, for the time when I shall sleep
Without identity,
And never care how rain may steep
Or snow may cover me!" [1]

Oblivion is all he asks. In his pride he rejects heaven and the hell of fire.

[1] The italics are from the original MS.

224

> *"No promised heaven, these wild desires*
> *Could all or half fulfil;*
> *No threatened hell, with quenchless fires,*
> *Subdue this quenchless will!"* [1]

Nothing but complete dominion of both, God's place, will do for him who asks surrender to his desire of the Holy Spirit, and seeks conquest of Heaven.

Once there was war in Heaven. Archangel Lucifer strove with God and was defeated and cast out. Desire for dominion of God is Lucifer's eternal punishment.

Lucifer has been an angel and, since his fall, has made conquest of Adam, God's created son whom he envies, for he envies all on whom God's love has ever shone. Thus while he cries with unquenched pride he also knows the inward strife of God and man and devil.

> "Three gods, within this little frame,
>   Are warring, night and day;
> Heaven could not hold them all, and yet
>   They all are held in me;
> And must be mine till I forget
>   My present entity!
> Oh, for the time, when in my breast
>   Their struggles will be o'er!
> Oh, for the day, when I shall rest,
>   And never suffer more!"

In his dark torment Satan is damned to behold the great vision, the vision of the universe about the feet of God. His eyes cry to his heart:

[1] The italics are from the original MS.

225

"I saw a spirit, standing, man,
   Where thou dost stand—an hour ago,
And round his feet three rivers ran,
   Of equal depth, and equal flow—
A golden stream—and one like blood;
   And one like sapphire seemed to be;
But where they joined their triple flood
   It tumbled in an inky sea.
The spirit sent his dazzling gaze
   Down through that ocean's gloomy night;
Then, kindling all, with sudden blaze,
   The glad deep sparkled wide and bright—
White as the sun, far, far more fair
   Than its divided sources were!"

Behold God, and Lucifer's vision of himself as God.
Behold the light of Heaven illuminating chaos.

"Even for that spirit seer" (cries Satan to his eyes),
   "I've watched and sought my lifetime long
Sought him in heaven, hell, earth, and air,
   An endless search, and always wrong.
 Had I but seen his glorious eye
   Once light the clouds that 'wilder me,
I ne'er had raised this coward cry
   To cease to think, and cease to be;
I ne'er had called oblivion blest
   Nor, stretching eager hands to death
Implored to change for senseless rest
   This sentient soul, this living breath.
Oh, let me die—that power and will
   Their cruel strife may close;
And conquered good and conquering ill
   Be lost in one repose!"

Satan cannot deny God because he has seen him, and cannot possess God because only by surrender is God to be possessed; and conquest of God, subjection of God is the essence of sin. Let God and Satan, therefore, be wiped out in utter oblivion and make an equal end of all things. He for whom no promised heaven of worship will suffice indeed must seek endlessly through heaven and hell and earth and air for God; and should he meet God he will meet him but to lose Him; to meet defeat, to be cast out again in the pride of his wild desire, and his quenchless will.

There is Hell.

This is the hell awaiting you and me, if we try to stand alone in our pride, if we expect the millennium to come to us like a tame dove and minister to our wants, to fill our pockets and bring us fame and give us love. Some of us, in rage that God is not our slave, have run away from the life we find barren of dominion, and others, in despair or pique or ignorance, seek petty distractions to fill the silent hours of our life.

I, Virgil, too, have been a man even as you, Dante. You and I visit this dark place together, and we see not one, but many Satans here, and all Satans only as one, the Dark Hero. Hail and Farewell, sir, may we not meet again in this fearful place where "the emperor of the woeful realm" lies in his icy bonds. "Oh, how great a marvel it seemed to me, when I saw three faces on his head! one in front, that was crimson; the others were two, which were joined to this above the very middle of each shoulder, and they were joined up to the

227

place of the crest; and the right was of a colour between white and yellow, and the left was such in appearance as those who come from there whence the Nile descends." These faces are the faces of Impotence, Ignorance and Hate, but they also are the faces of the defeated creator, lost humanity and love turned to hate. Well may you tremble, Dante, at the horrid vision, let us leave here together, and issue forth again "to see the stars."

XXXII

UNDER THE STARS

"O stars, and dreams, and gentle night;
O night and stars, return!
And hide me from the hostile light
That does not warm, but burn."

Emily Jane Brontë

THE human body in which this spirit was housed had yet to live a while, had to eat and drink and even be merry with a ghost of mirth. For three long years the miraculous courage which makes of this dark being a hero sustained him in the dungeon of his earthly life. For three more years his humanity fought fiercely with his princely darkness to remain on God's created earth.

His body dwelt at Haworth in kitchen and parlour and had human relatives as all bodies have, and breathed the air of day and saw the stars of night and knew very trivial necessities.

Thus bear with Charlotte and Anne and Branwell awhile yet; bear most of all with Branwell. These times will sound with strophe and antistrophe of magnificent music and with a Hymn to Satan. The voice of Satan will be uplifted in the wilderness in his own praise. He will sing his own damnation and eternal death.

229

Return to Charlotte at Hathersage, Charlotte who valued public opinion and grieved because those French newspapers had ceased to come. On her journey home to Haworth she met a Frenchman in the train and, just because he spoke the French tongue, addressed him. Charlotte, the shy, spoke to a strange man in a train because he was French.

When she got home, she found Branwell there, dismissed from the service of Mr. Robinson in disgrace. I think drink and opium and unfulfilled ambition had gone to his brain. He was always madly conceited, now a very mania of conceit possessed him. He believed a woman, his master's wife, was perishing for love of him and was but awaiting the death of her husband to endow him with her riches and her love. He imagined already that she, like Potiphar's wife, had offered him her honour.

In his youth he had been neglected and spoilt. He had been made a free present of a Future which he had not earned. All his closet companions were people of an inferior order from one point of view, girls and his father's parishioners. His precociousness made him conspicuous among men by years his seniors. Worst of all for a young man of somewhat feminine temperament he was reared in a house full of women, two of whom had wills that nothing could break, and one of these was his elder sister and counsellor and the sharer of his artistic life. Charlotte was Branwell's friend until he began to go wrong. Directly she began to suspect his goings on, she began to watch, one feels, to watch him, and gradually to grow more and more ashamed of him and more and more disgusted with him, until she could not speak to him or sit in the same room.

When Charlotte returned home in July she found Branwell ill; "he is so very often owing to his own fault. I was not therefore shocked at first, but when Anne informed me of the immediate cause of his present illness, I was greatly shocked." Thereupon Charlotte told Ellen Nussey that Mr. Robinson had written to him "sternly dismissing him, intimating that he had discovered his proceedings." Branwell took to drink and drugs as a solace and became so bad that he was sent away from home in charge of somebody. He wrote to Charlotte expressing "some sense of contrition for his frantic folly," and promised amendment on his return, but as long as he remained at home Charlotte "scarce dare hope for peace in the house."

All this is told to Ellen Nussey, all Branwell's private affairs.

In August Branwell recovered partly because he was now "*forced* to abstain," Charlotte having no doubt taken command of the situation. Emily and Anne regretted with her that Ellen could not be asked to stay while Branwell was at home—"while he is here—you shall not come. I am more confirmed in that resolution the more I know of him," wrote Charlotte. She hoped and very wisely urged, that he would get some employment until she began to fear that he had "rendered himself incapable of filling any respectable station in

231

life; besides if money were at his disposal . . ." But it was not. He was reduced to the lowest state of degradation, that of a hanger-on to his family. He was reduced to pledge his family's honour to get hold of what he craved. Pledge it he did, and in due course the sheriff's officers, bums as we call them in Yorkshire, paid visits to the Parsonage.

Then things came to such a pass that Charlotte dared not leave the house, for in her absence poor Branwell bluffed a sovereign out of old Brontë and went down and fuddled himself at the Black Bull. Emily gave the show away this time and called him a hopeless being to wind up her account.

Branwell himself wrote a very complete and romantic account of his case in October, 1845, to Francis H. Grundy his old friend, a great tale of illness and love, which lies Charlotte believed but did not pity him for, as the lady was married. This wild romance seems to have been a delusion of Branwell's condition.

The following May he again wrote to Mr. Grundy asking for a job. He said he was recovered and re-formed. Charlotte's letters show his continuing degeneration. Branwell asked honestly, I believe, for help to get a post—and as Mr. Grundy had seen him, according to this letter, in a state of "grovelling carelessness, the malignant yet cold debauchery, the determination to find how far mind could carry body without both being chucked into hell" and furthermore considering that his one-time employment at Luddenfoot had ended in a scandal which was hushed up, a scandal in which

232

the word embezzlement was hinted at, Mr. Grundy is to be congratulated on apparently offering him a post on the railway again which for some reason he did not take.

I will conclude the story of his delusion because of its bearing upon Emily's contemporary activities. There is considerable doubt in my mind as to whether Mrs. Robinson or Mr. Robinson ever knew of Branwell's adoration. Maybe it was only his addiction to drugs which came to the notice of the invalid Mr. Robinson. It is certain, however, that Mrs. Robinson did not return his infatuation. Branwell believed she did and kept letters of hers in his pocket we are told. Whose letters they really were does not signify, if any there were. People have been known to write to themselves in like madnesses. Branwell believed that the lady would, on Mr. Robinson's expected death, fling "herself and estate" into his arms. Mr. Robinson died on May 26th, 1846. Mrs. Robinson refrained from Branwell's embrace. Branwell said Mr. Robinson had arranged his will in such a way that his widow would lose all if she so much as saw Branwell or held any communication with him. His will was proved in September, 1846, and therein Mrs. Robinson's freedom was not restricted in any way. Clement Shorter possessed a copy of this document, and it is from his collection of the letters of the Brontës that I derive this statement.

To Branwell the *news* that Mr. Robinson had altered his will before he died so as effectively to prevent, "all

233

chance of a marriage between his widow [aged forty-five or forty-six] and Branwell," came in June some three months before the will was proved. Branwell became "intolerable," allowed old Brontë, with whom he still slept, "rest neither day nor night," screwed money out of him, and sometimes threatened to kill himself if he did not get it. He said Mrs. Robinson had gone insane. He refused good situations which Charlotte averred were offered him, and did nothing but drink. Charlotte at this point did wonder for a moment if Branwell were altogether speaking the truth; but afterwards, it would seem Mrs. Robinson became the Designing Woman, that stand-by of all females with unhappy brothers to account for: "a worse woman hardly exists," said Charlotte hereafter. How far was Charlotte speaking the truth? Charlotte Brontë was not a liar. In so far as she knew, and in so far as her wishes allowed her to know, she told the truth, both about Branwell and this lady, but people do not always know what they see. Her opinion of Branwell expressed to Ellen Nussey must always be read with this in mind. Outwardly, and as far as she was able to make herself, as far as she saw the necessity of it for human conduct, Charlotte was strict and orthodox. The longer she lived, the more so she became. When Branwell went astray she was shocked. From that point she seems to have treated him as one who had no right to rule or try to rule himself. She tried to rule him herself. Apparently she ruled without sympathy. Her remarks concerning

234

him are doubtless true from her point of view. But of course there is another side to the case. There is more myth grown up about Branwell than about any of his sisters. I cannot, therefore, attempt to present his side of the case. One can imagine that a man of his temperament, emotional, violently in need of stimulation of one kind or another, had not much chance before Charlotte, his elder sister, in the dull little village of Haworth. Emily and Anne stood with Charlotte to all intents and purposes. This man slept with that old parson, his father, a parson's son "gone wrong" he was, one of the most unfortunate beings on earth.

In her heart Emily alone felt deeply for Branwell. She wrote him at least one poem:

> "How few, of all the hearts that loved,
>   Are grieving for thee now;
> And why should mine to-night be moved
>   With such a sense of woe?"

Even she, though, called him a wanderer from the fold and believed the Robinson story.

> "It recks not now, when all is over:
>   But yet my heart will be
> A mourner still, though friend and lover
>   Have both forgotten thee!"

Alas, during this early part of his decline, she called him a "hopeless being" and carried tales of him to Charlotte. Perhaps in life, Heathcliff did really triumph over Hindley Earnshaw's fall.

235

Heathcliff is not Branwell. You have only to read Emily's poems to see her totally different attitude toward his sufferings and those of her brother. Heathcliff is herself. I say this now, reiterate it, in order to remove any suspicion in your mind that Branwell's ravings were the model for his. When Branwell, according to his lights, found himself deserted and deceived by Mrs. Robinson about May 26th, *Wuthering Heights* was almost certainly finished. It was so far in preparation on April 6th that Charlotte spoke of it to her publishers. By the beginning of August, it had visited sundry publishers and the first proofs were in the press. Heathcliff's rage against Catherine, which is but the old rage of the Dark Hero in Emily's poems, must have been written (it occurs in the first half of the book) before Branwell broke out against Mrs. Robinson.

I feel this is in a sense unnecessary, because Heathcliff could rage well enough in his own tongue without the aid of borrowed accents.

But I want to still, if possible, those minds who see Branwell as the model for Heathcliff, or Heathcliff as Branwell's image of himself as the betrayed lover. Some may say that Branwell was acting out in his life the romance he had already written, but that is far-fetched. Besides, I repeat, Emily had already written out the passion of this book in her poems.

I am not going to engage any further in the "Branwell" controversy, the controversy that he wrote *Wuthering Heights*. If at the end of this book, any doubt exists in your mind that Emily could or did write it, this book is worthless. I make an end of that matter here as far as I am concerned, and for the time being, an end of Branwell.

XXXIII

A REVELATION. CHARLOTTE DISCOVERS
EMILY'S PRIVATE LIFE AND ARRANGES
FOR ITS PUBLICATION

"Our corn was garnered months before,
Threshed out and harvested with gore;

.   .   .   .   .   .

I, doubly cursed on foreign sod
Fought neither for my home nor God."
Emily Jane Brontë

BRANWELL'S affair was not the only business which agitated the women of the Brontë family in the twelve months between July, 1845, and July, 1846.

To go back to 1845, on July 30th, 1845, according to Emily's date, on the 31st to be precise, a few days after Branwell's dismissal from employment and return home, and just after Charlotte's return from Hathersage, Emily and Anne wrote each other a one-day diary. Emily's diary is a direct contradiction of her poems. "I am quite contented for myself: not as idle as formerly altogether as hearty, . . . merely desiring that everybody could be as comfortable as myself and as undesponding." Her poem, written in private about this date and obviously concerning the family, is called *The Captive's Lament,* and ends:—

238

"Better that I, my own fate mourning,
   Should pine alone in this prison gloom,
Than waken free on the summer morning,
   And feel they were suffering this awful doom."

The chief part of the paper refers to past history that we already know, and a journey, "our first long journey by ourselves together" which she and Anne took to York, and on which they played the Gondal game. I have no idea why they went to York, but they enjoyed themselves very much, save for a few hours at Bradford. All at home are in decent health but B., though Papa has a complaint of the eyes. She hopes B. "will be better and do better hereafter." The paper concludes with an account of the lives and deaths of various cats, dogs, etc. Anne's paper is the counterpart of this save for the information that Charlotte is thinking about taking another situation and wants to go to Paris. Emily is engaged in writing the Emperor Julius's life. "She is writing some poetry too. I wonder what it is about?" The Gondal game, according to Anne, is not in first-class playing order.

It is interesting to see how Emily wished to appear to her family, interesting to see how Emily conceived of herself from their point of view—a child apparently a player of games, a perfectly cheerful ironer of linen.

There is the mask, the convention. Neither Charlotte nor Anne in private were deceived by it. One has to protect oneself with something in family life. Emily, aged twenty-seven, writes for her sister as if she were ten years old. Anne saw the real Emily behind

239

this blade of grass. Charlotte saw a closed door. When Charlotte tried to get behind this blade of grass to open the door, she found it was a bar of steel.

One day in the winter of 1845-46, a misfortune befell Emily. Charlotte accidentally discovered her poems and, not accidentally, read them.

"My sister Emily was not a person of demonstrative character, nor one on the recesses of whose mind and feelings even those nearest and dearest to her could, with impunity, intrude unlicensed: it took hours to reconcile her to the discovery I had made."

Nothing to my mind can excuse this action of Charlotte's. Why was Emily reconciled if she were ever reconciled, you may ask? Water will wear away a stone. Stoics give up fights they cannot end. Charlotte won and peace of sorts was made. Charlotte continued the battle. Some of these poems must be published, she declared.

It took "days to persuade her that such poems merited publication. I knew, however, that a mind like hers could not be without some latent spark of honourable ambition, and refused to be discouraged in my attempts to fan that spark to flame."

Honourable ambition! There is a great gulf between Charlotte's "honourable ambition" and the "wild desires" of the philosopher. Her carefully preserved "incognito," *Emily Jane Brontë*, sister and laundress, was destroyed. Those that had eyes to see could now behold. Charlotte saw; but how much she saw Heaven alone knows.

Caroline Helstone said of Shirley:—

"At dead of night; when all the house was silent, and starlight, and the cold reflection from the snow glimmered in our chamber—then I saw Shirley's heart . . . like a shrine—for it was holy; like snow—for it was pure; like flame—for it was warm; like death—for it was strong."

Charlotte called Emily after she was dead "stronger than a man, simpler than a child." In so far as her love of Emily permitted her to go, her epitaph is right, but I am forced to take other of Charlotte's words and add them to this praise, words Charlotte spoke of Heathcliffe: "but tyranny and ignorance made of him a mere demon."

I am sure that Charlotte began to love Emily after this discovery in a new way, with admiration and passion, with fear and pity. As time went on Emily became heroic for her as the dead are heroic, and as a hero Emily has lived through Charlotte's words, as a man bravely fighting life's battles, and in the end fighting death. Yet nevertheless one has to destroy that gallant figure, called in soldier language Major and Captain by her sister. Greater heroism and more dauntless courage than Charlotte ever imagined supported this soul on her long journey outward from human life.

Emily haunted Charlotte after this discovery, before and after she was dead, not as ghosts do, but not unlike ghosts do, and Charlotte tried to lay that spirit by offering it wealth and independence and the final comfort of complete surrender in love. *Shirley* is Charlotte's worst book, and yet it is a brave book. In it she tried to show what riches and homage and love might have made of "Major" Brontë. "Captain" Keeldar is Charlotte's reparation offered by the living to the dead, and something more. It is Charlotte's refusal to accept the bitter truth.

I hate to write the rest of this book in which Charlotte's love began to dawn too late. Very difficult it is to write of the inner things of life, to write of love that is come too late, that is born of a discovery which stinks of betrayal, for Charlotte got past Emily's reserve by something very much akin to treachery. She pried into a life that had defended itself against intrusion for twenty long years. Her wish to know, to guide, to manage were too strong for her; and she never felt, I believe, that she had no right to discover what she did, and no shadow of a right to arrange the affairs of another's innermost heart.

Fortunately, full revelation of this life did not at once dawn upon her; but I think perhaps something near full revelation did come to her slowly while Emily was yet a body upon earth; and after, when her body was dead. Else why did she destroy, as she seems to have destroyed, every private paper of Emily's but a few poems? Letters and all are gone, and Anne's letters too, all are gone, everything of Emily's and everything of her one close friend's, the friend who wrote *The Three Guides*, wherein any one that reads may recognize that she knew the darkness and the pride in Emily's breast.

242

And why did Charlotte write *Shirley?* I have said as a reparation from the living and as a refusal to accept the bitter truth.

Yes, twice Charlotte denied Emily, twice refused to accept her as she was, and gave to the world willingly only a few edited and altered poems, and a new-created Emily made up of what she loved in her and of what she wished Emily might have been.

The real Emily was contrary to all that Charlotte struggled for. Charlotte struggled to accept, Emily refused. Charlotte tried her utmost to conform to the world as it presented itself to her, the world of normal everyday men and women. With this world Emily had nothing whatever to do. Charlotte had a sense of "right," she knew what was right and could not cease to try and inflict her code on others. Had she not taught Emily and Anne the rudiments of French and grammar? Even so she tried to teach them the A. B. C. of this world.

This is all terrible tragedy. I cannot help it. Emily's life was one of the most terrible tragedies on earth.

It took Charlotte a long while to overcome Emily and get her permission for publication of a few poems with a batch of her own and a few of Anne's. These poems were printed at private cost by Messrs. Aylott and Jones. That little book, *Poems of Currer, Ellis, and Acton Bell*, 1846, contained only twenty-one of Ellis's private experiences, edited and altered here and there by Charlotte. Ellis passed the alterations. Why not? Why struggle, why fight? Having given up one's most treasured possession, one's secret soul, why stick at a few words?

XXXIV

WEIRD TALES

By E. T. W. Hoffmann and Ellis Bell

*"Who does not know with what mysterious power
the mind is enthralled in the midst of unusual and
singularly strange circumstances? Even the dullest
imagination is aroused when it comes into a valley
girt around by fantastic rocks, or within the gloomy
walls of a church or an abbey, and it begins to have
glimpses of things it has never yet experienced."*
                    The Entail. E. T. W. Hoffmann

*"What have those lonely mountains worth revealing?
More glory and more grief than I can tell:
The earth that wakes one human heart to feeling
Can centre both the worlds of Heaven and Hell."*
                    Stanzas. Emily Jane Brontë

NOT long after the discovery of Emily's poems the three sisters decided to write three tales, to form together one of those sets of three volumes in which the public liked to have fiction served to it.

They sat down together in the parlour every evening alone by themselves and in secret, night after night in the fashion of Scheherezade, spun their yarns until each had woven a complete romance. Romance I say, but Anne wrote of her governess life, and Charlotte wrote of Brussels, and Emily wrote of the moors, and each of

245

the three figured as hero or heroine or both of her own tale.

Nobody knew of this nightly writing, and nobody knew of the poems, not even Ellen Nussey. In this manner *The Professor* and *Agnes Grey* and *Wuthering Heights* came into being during the winter and spring of 1845-46.

A deal of time and labour has been spent on trying to show the "origin" of *Wuthering Heights*.[1] It seems to be obvious enough. The form to begin with, the framework of *this story of an Entail* was borrowed outright from *The Entail* by E. T. W. Hoffmann.

There Hoffmann told the story of a visit to a lonely castle on a deserted moor. After an historic preamble, for which Emily substituted the past history of the reader's friend Mr. Lockwood, two men, the narrator and he who is to tell the real story within this story, visit an old castle at night in a snowstorm, where an old servant of extraordinary figure lets them in after considerable ado. The younger of these men, the narrator, spends his first evening reading a gruesome volume, Schiller's *Ghost-Seer*, which reading is followed by a nightmare in which he hears "sighing and moaning at intervals, and in this sighing and moaning there was expressed the deepest trouble, the most hopeless grief, that a human being can know." These sounds are accompanied by a scratching on the wall as of some imprisoned animal.

[1] See Appendix V.

I cannot relate the story of a hundred pages that unfolds the mystery of this ghostly beginning, the story of Old Daniel, the servant, with his peculiar temper and crooked devotion to the family of von R——. It would take too long. It is a tale of passionate love and bitter feelings, of a usurper and an orphan heir. The R—— family history is connected with two houses, one this gloomy castle, and one a fine estate in Courland, note that. Note too, that the orphan heir of the gloomy castle marries the orphan heiress of Courland. Have I roused your curiosity enough to read *The Entail*, to hearken to the wind howling in a solemn dirge above the groaning fir-trees that stood about the old castle of R——sitten?

None can fail to recognize in Daniel the cross-grained house steward, own brother to Joseph of *Wuthering Heights*, rigged out in grander garments, but with the same feudal crooked fidelity to the head of the house, dead or alive. There is the sane old man of law too, who relates the story within this story who has his counterpart in Nellie Dean of Emily's tale. The heroine is a beautiful young wife who suffers from "morbid excitability, which will finally destroy all the happiness of her life."

No more will I say except that Emily quickly found Mr. Lockwood the narrator of *her* tale, of little use to her and, having employed him as a laborious means of conducting the reader to the Heights, put him to bed of pneumonia and only allowed him to play the part of Hoffmann's narrator in very cut down and reduced

247

circumstances. Nellie Dean, on the other hand, the faithful counsellor, has a greater place in her story than Hoffmann's man of law.

Wuthering Heights was to be a tale and not a novel, and I think Emily set off at the start to emulate that great writer of tales, Hoffmann. But she lived her story, whereas he is outside of his, and thus, though she kept to his form, her story grew with a new life and after its own fashion upon his skeleton, and her characters arose in their own strength upon the bones of his. Joseph emerges from the tomb of Daniel, Nellie Dean takes upon her the job of the old estate lawyer, Catherine Earnshaw replaces Seraphina, and the younger Catherine more than fills the little part of the younger Seraphina. Heathcliff is cousin in darkness of the soul of the R—— family, a soul that had dealings with the devil and the black arts.

The story, however, that grew out of all this is no tale of a feudal family's quarrels; it is the history of that waif of no parentage, that dark and mournful child who found himself cast upon a moor among strangers. There he met his soul and worshipped it; and there his soul and he went, first soul and then body down to the grave and damnation in the pride of his strength. By his own will he quitted this world and heaven, in soul and in body. By his own wild desire he cast himself out for ever, cast himself out upon the moor, and on the edge of the moor his body was buried without benefit of clergy and his unrepentant ghost they said, walked hand in hand with his soul upon the moor.

248

XXXV

"WUTHERING HEIGHTS"

"Heathcliffe, again, of Wuthering Heights, *is quite another creation. He exemplified the effects which a life of continued injustice and hard usage may produce on a naturally perverse, vindictive, and inexorable disposition, carefully trained and kindly treated, the black gipsy-cub might possibly have been reared into a human being, but tyranny and ignorance made of him a mere demon. The worst of it is, some of his spirit seems breathed through the whole narrative in which he figures: it haunts every moor and glen, and beckons in every fir-tree of the* Heights."
C. Brontë to W. S. Williams, Esq.,
August 14th, 1848.

"Ellis has a strong, original mind, full of strange though sombre power. When he writes poetry that power speaks in language at once condensed, elaborated, and refined, but in prose it breaks forth in scenes which shock more than they attract. Ellis will improve, however, because he knows his defects."
C. Bell to W. S. Williams, Esq.,
December 21st, 1847.

AT last, the long journey is concluded and I am come to Wuthering Heights. Farewell to Charlotte and to Hoffmann, to Branwell and old Brontë, and the whole pack of cards.

The moors arise on all sides, the moor wind blows,

and there on the horizon stands a long stone house. "One may guess the power of the north wind blowing over the edge," as we call the moor-crest, "by the excessive slant of a few stunted firs at the end of the house; and by a range of gaunt thorns all stretching their limbs one way, as if craving alms of the sun." The date "1500" is carved over the door among "crumbling griffins and shameless little boys." The house is strongly built, "the narrow windows are deeply set in the wall, and the corners defended with large jutting stones."

Wuthering Heights stands solitary upon the moor. In other solitudes of the moor stand other Wuthering Heights. Well I know one with a garden before it not worth the name, and the heath about its western wall. There, for the sake of savage neighbours, the great door into the living-room, "they call it here 'the house' pre-eminently," the door from the world without into the world within, is only five feet high, and there is a step down on the threshold so that strangers have to bow the head and watch their feet, while the master of the place decides whether to hit them on the head or bid them welcome.

There you have the spirit of our country, a spirit that is not yet dead.

Into this house of Wuthering Heights came, in the first year of last century—the era of this tale is a convention, Hoffmann's era—an unwelcome stranger. He came on business, but the snow began to fall about him and he was stranded and had to stay one night to dream a dream. He was put to rest in an old box-bed in a disused room. A window of the room was also a window of the bed; and as he placed his candle on the window ledge he saw the names Catherine Earnshaw, Catherine Linton, Catherine Heathcliff scratched all over the paint. He found an Old Testament inscribed "Catherine Earnshaw, her book," and therein on a blank page a portion of a diary, Catherine Earnshaw's diary of her childish contentions with Joseph, the still living servant of the house. Therein it appeared that Joseph set about to save the souls of Miss Cathy, and her companion Heathcliff "the unhappy plough-boy," but Miss Cathy reaved "th' back off 'Th' Helmet o' Salvation' un' Heathcliff's pawsed his fit into t' first part o' "T'Brooad Way to Destruction'," Joseph's manuals of conversion. Joseph asserted that "owd Nick" would fetch them as sure as they were living.

The stranger, Mr. Lockwood, fell asleep upon this diary and dreamed a dream. No matter here of the first part of it. In the second part he dreamed of a voice that cried at the window " 'Let me in—let me in' and a scratching on the pane 'Let me in!' and a child's face looking through the dark pane. 'Let me in!', 'It is twenty years, twenty years. I've been a waif for twenty years!' " There is Emily at the window, a small pale child scratching to get in to love.

"Thus it was one festal night, When I was hardly six years old"—since when Emily also for twenty years or more, has been a waif, "lone, wholly lone."

The twenty years are shed away and behold Catherine Earnshaw the child at home at Wuthering Heights, a

251

dark handsome little thing with her foster-sister small Nellie Dean, her elder brother Hindley and her stern old father. There is also a mother of no interest and that same crooked man servant Joseph.

Into this family was brought, when Catherine "was hardly six years old," a waif, a "dirty, ragged, black-haired child" a thing of no country or parentage. Mr. Earnshaw was in a sense its father since he found and adopted it. Cathy and Heathcliff (as it was named both for "Christian and surname") soon became "very thick."

Thus the Hero arrived, the Dark Hero of mysterious parentage, of birth clouded in myth like the heroes of old. Who knew but his father was Emperor of China and his mother an Indian Queen? Not to the end of time shall we know who this creature's parents were, whether he was created along with the universe out of chaos or was a primordial darkness.

Not long after Heathcliff's arrival in the Earnshaw family, the children took ill of the measles and he with them. Hardness, not gentleness, made him give little trouble to his nurse. Cathy loved him more and more as time went on and Mr. Earnshaw doted upon him at the expense of Catherine's brother Hindley. He never repaid the old man's kindness by any sign of gratitude.

Then Hindley went from home and the old man died.

After this Heathcliff's dominion was over and Hindley came back with a young wife to oppress and crush him in revenge for the love old Earnshaw bore him. No degradation was spared the sullen proud boy. He was made the drudge of the farm. This degradation he supported for the sake of Catherine's presence, in worship of Catherine who dominated his black heart.

Came a day when this pair in one of their adventures on the moor ran as far as Thrushcross Grange, the big house of the district, where the rich Lintons, landlords of many acres, lived. Heathcliff and Cathy got in the park and ran up to the house to see how the Linton children, Edgar and Isabel, spent their Sunday evenings. They found an uncurtained window and looking in at it saw a splendid crimson-and-white drawing-room as beautiful as paradise. But the little Lintons inside were quarrelling.

As they clung to the window ledge staring in, the Lintons heard them and in fright howled for Papa and Mamma. Folk stirred, doors were opened, and a great bull-dog was set on the intruders. He got hold of Cathy and gripped her. It was, of course, found that his prey was Miss Earnshaw, the Lintons' neighbour, and she was thereupon taken into that crimson heaven to be cured and cossetted, *but Heathcliff was left in outer darkness.*

As the years passed, the Linton influence got hold of Catherine's heart; her love for Heathcliff waged war in her with love of what that red drawing-room signified and what the fair haired Linton signified. In the end it came to this, that Edgar Linton became her fair lover and she gave him her word. She deserted Heathcliff for worldly riches and the fair lover.

But in what frame of mind was she while acting thus?

253

Did she seek Linton to surrender to him, because she found in him the happiness of her life? Indeed not. She determined on Linton's surrender to her. This fair lover was to be her creature and her thing, to use and to hold for Heathcliff and herself. Were not she and Heathcliff one? At this moment in the face of her marriage with her fair lover, she cried of Heathcliff— "he's more myself than I am. Whatever our souls are made of, his and mine are the same." "What were the use of my creation, if I were entirely contained here?" [striking her breast.] "My great miseries in this world have been Heathcliff's miseries, and I watched and felt each from the beginning: my great thought in living is himself. If all else perished, and *he* remained, *I* should still continue to be; and if all else remained, and he were annihilated, the universe would turn to a mighty stranger . . . I *am* Heathcliff! He's always, always in my mind: not as a pleasure, any more than I'am always a pleasure to myself, but as my own being."

She had, alas, said before she spoke these words that it would degrade her to marry Heathcliff. Heathcliff heard that and went. He heard that and no more and therewith disappeared, vanished back into the night from whence he came. Catherine, the soul that loved him, that was one with him, had betrayed him for the world, for the ghost of the fair lover.

When Catherine found that Heathcliff was gone from her, she fell ill of despair, but between roughness and indulgence she recovered and lived to domineer and torment her fellows for three years. This illness set her apart from and above her friends and relatives. From now she obeyed no laws that ruled the lives of ordinary mortals. Her whim was all she sought in life, and her whim led her to marry Edgar Linton.

Linton was her slave, her Fancy, her Fairy Love, I well believe. After her marriage, she showed an almost foolish fondness for him as long as he was perfectly obedient and complacent.

All might have gone on pleasantly enough; this happy season, marred with intervals of gloom on Catherine's part, might have long continued, but shortly after her marriage Heathcliff came back from his mysterious wanderings. The morose boy came back from the unknown grown into a man, dark and heroic in aspect. Where had he been? In the Army? Had he finished his education on the Continent? He had certainly been in hell and emerged out of the shades, when he heard that his living soul had given herself in marriage, only to bid her farewell, to settle his score with Hindley Earnshaw and to put an end to himself.

But Catherine showed ecstasy at his return, became breathlessly wild, not with gladness, "indeed, by her face, you would rather have surmised an awful calamity," and fixed her gaze on him "as if she feared he would vanish." Her demon-lover had come back.

Heathcliff showed caution at first, in public at least, but straightway renounced the idea of swift revenge and self-destruction. He set himself instead to make life bow to his control. He set himself partly out of

255

revenge, partly out of pure lust for power, to annihilate the Earnshaw and Linton families.

Now Catherine, Heathcliff's living soul, his mind, his earthly counterpart, set out to bait her fair lover Linton as a frenzied hound baits a bull. Linton was not of that kind. He was but a whim of hers, and a whim will not strive against the mind that created it, but will faint and go. Catherine tried to strive against Linton, to rouse him to do battle that she might conquer him again. There was nothing to conquer. Linton was only a ghost, a Fancy, a Fairy Love, and not the true bright spirit. Linton, her creature, failed her. The spirit she sought in Heaven, hell, earth and air was not in him. By every means in her power she tried to urge him to do battle with herself and with Heathcliff, to fight her demon. On the result of that battle hung her choice, but a mere whim will not fight and cannot conquer anything. Nay, though Ellis Bell had himself recognized the true significance of Linton, the fair lover, the symbol of the white spirit of God; even so, neither Ellis Bell nor Catherine could have urged him up to mortal combat, for this spirit does not engage himself at the devil's provocation in contest for dominion. He has fought the devil once and for all, and now turns the other cheek or goes unconquerable away.

In fury that she could not rouse Linton up, Catherine tried to die before his eyes, to go out to the grave, there to await Heathcliff, there to be one with him for ever. Her soul would embrace her damned soul in the grave, and her heart should lie there along with her demon-heart careless of Heaven or hell. In the madness of her disappointment over Linton Catherine did her mad best to die. One piercing cold day she flung open the window of her room and let death in upon her aching body from the moor.

Now began that song from human soul to demon-lover. Catherine had thrown the world and Heaven aside, and had no desire but a wild passion to be completely possessed. Heathcliff cried back fiercely of that old betrayal wherewith Catherine his living soul had betrayed him. He cursed her for traitor and murderer, for murderer of herself, of his life, his soul; he cursed her never to leave him, to haunt him, to torment him, and to suffer in the grave the hellish unrest and torment that tortured himself.

Demon to Demon; reckless of anything but themselves, these two sang the song of the Dark Hero's glory in himself, his utter worship of himself, his fury against self-betrayal. Mad that he had not found Heaven on earth to overcome it and possess it, he cast aside his search for the beauty of Heaven, and rejected earth.

Down to the grave, to oblivion the Dark Hero sought to go by his own hand. First the living soul shook off the body. "Oh, God!" cried Heathcliff to Catherine, "would *you* like to live with your soul in the grave?" "I *cannot* live without my soul."

At the last, when his living soul left him alone in the world, he feared she had escaped him. "May she wake in torment!" he cursed. . . . "I pray one prayer —I repeat it till my tongue stiffens—Catherine Earnshaw, may you not rest as long as I am living! . . . Be with me always—take any form—drive me mad!"

"Oh! could I see thy lids weighed down in cheerless woe;
 Too full to hide their tears; too stern to overflow;
 Oh! could I know thy soul with equal grief was torn,
 This fate might be endured, this anguish might be borne."

Long ago Emily Brontë wrote that poem; long ago her demon-lover had cried these words in the night of loneliness:—

" . . . if there be a God above
 Whose arm is strong, Whose word is true,
 This hell shall wring thy spirit too!"

Heathcliff's curse was fulfilled. As he lived through the long years wreaking his vengeance on the world, Catherine haunted about Wuthering Heights, outcast, crying against the window within which he and she had slept in each other's arms in childhood. "Let me in, let me in." "It is twenty years, twenty years. I've been a waif for twenty years." His soul haunted him, lost, utterly lost. His lost soul haunted him from that grave which was "already more than mine." His heart was dead, "unwept-for let the body go."

It was part of his damnation that he had to stay from the grave to level this world to his will. Not until Life had indeed bowed to his control and become his slave, and therefore dust and nothing in his hands, could he depart again to outer darkness. Not until he had won all his world, and as the devil must, found all, not being

258

God, was nothing, did he destroy the body about him. When this motive no longer held him he departed. A strange change came over him. He began to fade out of life, not as a flower fades. His body fought to remain on earth, but his ghost grew pale in his body. The total annihilation of that world he hated and had conquered no longer held him. There was nothing for him to annihilate. What he had won he had lost. His ghost paused on the threshold of death to dispose of his body. It was to be laid close against that other body, over against the moor, no wood or lead between them, but dust to dust and bone to bone. "No minister need come; nor need anything be said over me.—I tell you I have nearly attained *my* heaven; and that of others is altogether unvalued and uncoveted by me."

His body died in frightful exaltation upon that bed with the little window in it. The window was open, the rain streamed down upon him, but his ghost was gone to that other Ghost to walk upon the moor. There in freedom He and She and Liberty had undisputed sovereignty, there by the grace of God they wandered and wander still, but only by the grace of God. Heathcliff was buried as he wished, close against his soul's body without benefit of clergy.

"Shed no tears o'er that tomb,
   For there are angels weeping;
Mourn not him whose doom
   Heaven itself is mourning.

.   .   .   .   .

259

"The time of grace is past,
  And mercy, scorned and tried,
Forsakes to utter wrath at last
  The soul so steeled by pride."

Nevertheless, you, the stranger tell how you "lingered around" those tombs under the benign sky of September. The church in the graveyard was falling to ruin, the wind and the moor were reclaiming it and its dead. You "watched the moths fluttering among the heath and harebells, listened to the soft wind breathing through the grass, and wondered how any one could ever imagine unquiet slumbers for the sleepers in that quiet earth?"

If that is all you felt and saw, then you are fortunate. Long may the blessing of peace be yours. But as you crossed the moor did you not hear the grouse cry "Go back! Go back!" and the peewits wail, and the soft footsteps of the lost trail after you over the heather?

XXXVI

REFLECTIONS

THERE is Emily's life. Whether she died as Heathcliff died is not for you or me to judge. In due time I will tell you the manner of her death, how her body died and was buried; but whither her spirit went, or how it left this world, is not our business.

Surely *Wuthering Heights* is not Emily's life? There will be many who say that, even after this slow and painful unwinding of her history. It is. It is her autobiography, the life of her soul on earth from that time when she was "barely six years old" to the time when her poems were discovered.

Consciousness came to Emily in the form of Heathcliff, a dark waif of no clime, or country, or parentage. From the moment he came she began to lead a double life, his life, and the life of Catherine. How early he got the name of Heathcliff I do not know. It does not matter. There he was in her, perfectly unresponsive to her intimates, and until he showed himself to those intimates, in her imagination she was able to give him first place in her family. But he did show himself in her to those about her, and then he began to suffer. Every favour Branwell had tortured him. Because he

261

did not hold that place, he degraded himself into "a vicious cur" that hated "all the world as well as the kicker" for the indignities he felt put upon him. He degraded himself also into a drudge. Emily, however, in her other self was loved. Her sisters, at least were as fond of her as the Lintons were of Catherine. Out of their happy life the Heathcliff part of her was shut. He went from bad to worse and began to brood vengeance against her family and the world in general. His craving to be first to rule, to dominate, his craving for wealth and riches and love, wreaked itself upon his body. He continued to make that body slave for those he hated with black, frightful hate. In absolute loneliness but for his other self, Emily the loved, he slaved and cursed.

Emily was not averse to the pleasures denied him, though they meant nothing to her when she was in his mood. Human society had its charms for her. She even found the Edgar Lintons of this world, not beneath her interest, the fair Weightman did not disgust her.

At last there came a period of comparative happiness in Emily's life, at least retrospectively, and she forsook Heathcliff, her Dark Hero, forsook and betrayed him, but *he*, though miserable, did not desert her. His voice cried aloud to her:—

"Light up thy halls! Think not of me;
Absent is that face which thou hast hated so to see."

Though his miseries had been her miseries from the beginning, though he was herself in soul and body she

262

hated and loathed this creature she adored as only women can hate and loathe their demon-lover.

Then Emily discovered the world was vain. Against her heart she convinced herself it was a foul and empty thing, because she was disappointed in it. She wanted happiness and beauty and love, love beyond everything, but happiness she could not grasp, beauty she found only in loneliness on the moor and love, love of the dimension she desired was not anywhere on earth. Into her loneliness Heathcliff came back, he returned in his full power, in the power of the Dark Hero and took possession of her. He came on the heels of Fancy, her fair lover, that ghost of heavenly brightness which she had conjured up to comfort her solitude.

The family servant, the drudge, was separated from her and became Nellie Dean, a responsible and sane woman. Catherine died in her, and Emily became within nothing but the Dark Hero, Heathcliff.

Then she wrote *The Philosopher* and *Wuthering Heights.*

At Catherine's death in *Wuthering Heights,* the autobiography comes to an end. Then Emily did a curious thing, she re-wrote the story as it might have been without Heathcliff as hero. The hero is Hareton Earnshaw, the drudge, degraded but not vindictive; the heroine Catherine, only child of a wealthy father. Branwell was no longer Hindley Earnshaw in whose fall and decline Heathcliff took such pleasure, but the weak and feeble Linton Heathcliff, Heathcliff's puppet of a son. Both this Catherine and Hareton suffer through this

263

puppet. He gets her property in right of marriage and Hareton's place in right of mortgage. Then he dies and Catherine subsequently reclaims Hareton from the savagery he has fallen into. Heathcliff stands above all this might-have-been, working to destroy it till in the end he perceives it means nothing to him, that it did not exist, and never could have existed. Emily completed the vision dear to her imagination, and ended the story as she wished it could have ended, but it was outside of her experience. Catherine the younger and Hareton break away from Wuthering Heights, and all comes to a happy fairy tale conclusion; but Heathcliff puts aside this nonsense and faces his fate as he sees it, which fate Emily foresaw as hers when she wrote *Wuthering Heights.*

Life is open to every wind that blows, the human heart is not steadfast in misery or joy. Though *Wuthering Heights* is Emily's autobiography, it does not take stock of many things, those things which make it impossible ever to present the whole of one man's life, be it one's own or another's. Only two winds blow through *Wuthering Heights,* the soft south wind that came from the region beloved of Branwell and Charlotte, that bore dreams, wealth and happiness; and the Gondal wind, breath of the icy region, the lonely region in which the tempests of Emily's secret history roared and strove.

I have said there came a period of comparative happiness in Emily's life, when Heathcliff in his simple terror was lost to her sight. Most poor happiness it was,

264

it coincided to my mind with the confusion of adolescence. She began to find other interests outside of
Heathcliff when she was about twelve, and later lost
sight of him though his voice cried darkly in her
through the confusion. He came back when she was
grown up and had emerged from the tangled wood of
that first death, the death of her childhood. We break
up and die in adolescence I say again, and our life
thereafter is a conscious effort to realize all that we were
before, all those first fine feelings both of joy and suffering we knew before the world got at us.

For some of us, at least, this is so. For Emily it certainly was. This period of comparative happiness when
she was divided from Heathcliff was also a period of
death. Her finest feelings were clouded by the world's
affairs and attractions. Memory was her muse, the
muse of the wanderer and the dreamer, only now and
then in the confusion the voice of Heathcliff called
out loud and clear, and his voice cried the curses of a
betrayed lover. She all this time was Childe Roland
seeking the dark tower she had known before. She
found it and peopled it with the creatures of her imagination, among which there sang one, her comforter, the
seraph voice of her childhood. But in the seraph's voice
a demon moaned, and on the seraph's track came the
devil, and at last Childe Roland became possessed of the
devil and sang the devil's song.

Heathcliff, Catherine, Emperor Julius, Childe Roland,
Nellie Dean, Emily Jane Brontë, Major Brontë, behold
the confusion. I confuse you on purpose. Neither you

265

nor I can say of any living soul "Ecce Homo!" It is not in our power to review from birth to death the intricate windings of one man's life. Only as he presents himself to us can we see a fellow creature. We can therefore neither damn nor save him, not knowing all.

The devil knows God better than we shall ever know one another, for he has dwelt in God. He knows the fear of God, and in the knowledge of that fear, can address Him face to face. And the devil is a hero, for having lost all, he can exalt his heroic loneliness.

"No coward soul is mine!"

If I say this is Satan's hymn to God what will you think? Emily has been allowed to die thus far with these words on her lips. They were spoken before she wrote *Wuthering Heights*. Having given forth this praise she wrote *Wuthering Heights*. At the end of *Wuthering Heights* there is calm, yes, calm after storm, peace after battle; but the Church of God is crumbling away and the moor is creeping over everything.

"No coward soul is mine
   No trembler in the world's storm troubled sphere.
  I see Heaven's glories shine
   And faith shines equal arming me from fear.

"O God within my breast,
   Almighty, ever-present Deity!
  Life, that in me hast rest,
   As I—Undying Life, have power in thee:

266

"Vain are the thousand creeds
    That move men's hearts, unutterably vain,
Worthless as withered weeds
    Or idlest froth amid the boundless main,

"To waken doubt in one
    Holding so fast by thy infinity,
So surely anchored on
    The steadfast rock of Immortality.

"With wide-embracing love
    Thy Spirit animates eternal years,
Pervades and broods above,
    Changes, sustains, dissolves, creates and rears.

"Though Earth and moon were gone
    And suns and universes ceased to be,
And Thou wert left alone,
    Every Existence would exist in thee.

"There is not room for Death,
    Nor atom that his might could render void,
Since Thou art Being and Breath,
    And what Thou art may never be destroyed."

There is Emily's poem of exaltation, Heathcliff died in exaltation. He died possessed of Catherine's ghost and soul. I raise this horrible suggestion with dread, I suggest now that that *is* Satan's hymn to God, to himself as God.

God within my breast, Almighty ever present Deity, vain are the thousand creeds that move the hearts of men to waken doubt in one holding so fast by Thine infinity, God Who has rest in me *in whom I have power!*

Heathcliff died in exaltation with a sneer on his lips. Vain are the thousand creeds, O God, in whom I have power to waken doubt of my eternal faith in myself.

I think Emily when she wrote this poem did not know what she wrote.[1]

Let us leave this matter hanging in the air. There we must leave it, but if your mind inclines to dark forebodings, remember her body is not yet dead, and that while the body lives there is no end to the soul. Take all these threads of life I have unravelled, into your hands and weave any pattern your heart dictates, but do not ever think you have made the final pattern of Emily's whole life. To see the whole of any man's history you must wait till the end of earthly time.

[1] The version quoted here is from a photograph given to me by Davidson Cook, Esq., of a MS. dated January 2nd, 1846, and published by him in *The Nineteenth Century and After* in August, 1926.

XXXVII

THE LAST PHASE

"Farewell, unbless'd, unfriended child,
I cannot bear to watch thee die!"
Emily Jane Brontë

WHAT a small matter it seems that during this time while Emily Brontë was writing *Wuthering Heights*, her father went quite blind of cataract. How he managed Branwell in that young man's wild moments as he is supposed to have done, one cannot imagine. All that I can say is that Branwell seems to have settled down after the "shock" of Mrs. Robinson's infidelity to him into a thorough-going rake. The bailiffs continued to call upon him, and though some one sent him money, he did not pay his debts therewith, but used it to pave his way down the primrose path. I imagine that Mr. Grundy or one of his other admirers sent him this cash, but Charlotte suggests otherwise. Mrs. Robinson was supposed to be his source of supply. At any rate Branwell made a career of deterioration, became the suave and oily reprobate in public and threw fits—delirium tremens, I suppose—when his excesses got the better of him.

A curious thing happened after Mr. Robinson's will was proved. Anne's late pupils, the Misses Robinson,

269

began to correspond with Anne; their letters showed great affection for "their mother, and never make any allusion intimating acquaintance with her errors," said Charlotte. This correspondence was kept from Branwell. After his death, these girls even came to the Parsonage.

His friends considered Branwell's notions about Mrs. Robinson a delusion, a madness, a monomania; some of his friends at least did, but Branwell communicated his affairs far and wide, and they lost nothing in the gossip they provoked.

In the meantime Emily and Charlotte went to Manchester to see about an operation on their father's eyes, and a week or two later, on August 25th, 1846, the operation was successfully performed. Emily and Anne remained at home alone with Branwell for about five weeks.

While Charlotte was attending on her father she began *Jane Eyre*. Of that book, enough has been said to fill several volumes. Suffice here to say that the sources of its inspiration are almost all known or easily surmised. My only contributions are these. The fire scene which has agitated readers for three generations seems to be got direct from that mine of inspiration used by Emily, *The Entail* of Hoffmann; and Fairfax Rochester, rescued from infamy by the heroine, belongs to the Heathcliff genus. That Charlotte wrote *Wuthering Heights* has indeed occupied the mind of certain persons, and it has been sought to prove it by a vast number of parallel quotations from the two books, of which quotations the similarity is startling. Charlotte had read *Wuthering Heights* before she wrote *Jane Eyre*. When genius drives the pen, questions of plagiarism do not hold a place of much importance. Therefore I leave it to others to total up Charlotte's debt to her sister's book.

To turn aside for a moment to the affairs of Currer, Ellis, and Acton Bell. Their volume of poems had been published sometime about the end of June, 1846. The book sold only two copies in the ensuing twelve months. Aylott and Jones were the original publishers of this volume. Subsequently it was taken over from them by Smith, Elder and Co.

In August *Wuthering Heights* and *Agnes Grey* seem to have been sent to press by Mr. Newby, a gentleman of whom Charlotte had very black things to say. They lay fallow for over a year in his keeping.

As for Reviews of the Poems, *The Critic, The Dublin University Magazine,* and *The Athenæum* seem alone to have given the authors any satisfaction. *The Athenæum* put the usual "shows promise" into somewhat flowery language for Ellis's benefit.

In the following year, as a last effort to dig the poems out of their neglected grave, Charlotte distributed copies among various writers of whom De Quincey was one. Nothing of interest befell these works of prose and verse until very late in 1847, by which time Currer Bell had risen to fame by the publication of *Jane Eyre.*

Though Emily, as far as we know, never undertook another prose work after she had finished *Wuthering*

Heights, Anne began sometime or other during 1847 *The Tennant of Wildfell Hall,* a book of real talent. I said before that doubt was cast in my mind as to whether Mr. Huntingdon, the villain of this piece, was intended for Branwell. When I read that Mrs. C——, the victim of that Mr. C—— at one time curate at Haworth, turned up again at the Parsonage on April 4th, 1847, with a fresh installment of her woes and sufferings, my doubt becomes almost a certainty. Probably Branwell's behaviour helped to fill out the character of the degenerate hero, but that Branwell was the complete origin of the dreadful husband in this story, I will not believe.

This book was published in 1848, after *Wuthering Heights* and *Agnes Grey* were out, by the same Mr. Newby, who it seems profited in an ungenerous if not dishonest manner by the remoteness and obscurity of his clients.

Emily has left no relics of literary activity after her completion of *Wuthering Heights* save a few poems.

One of these is a fragment evidently begun as a comment on the Chartist disturbances which agitated the district until drastic measures were taken for their suppression in May, 1848. This fragment, beginning *It was the autumn of the year,* seems from internal evidence to be the basis of one of the last poems she ever wrote, namely *Why ask to know what date, what clime?* dated now May 15th, 1848. Mr. Hatfield hesitated when he gave this poem the date 1843 owing to an ill-made figure eight. It is under that date in the *Complete Poems* of 1923, the first stanza of *It was the autumn of*

272

the year appears in stronger form as the last three verses
of *Why ask to know?* The fragment smells of Hell Fire
the poem ends with a couplet to herself:—

> "I, doubly cursed on foreign sod,
>   Fought neither for my home nor God."

Time may perhaps reveal other poems of hers which
may correct the impression of darkness and lurid light
left by these few stanzas. Her very last poem, it is surmised, was that elegy to her brother which I have already
quoted from, *The Wanderer from the Fold.* A dreary,
weary thing it is.

There is very little more to say of the events of this
last phase of Emily's life. *Jane Eyre* was published in
October, 1847, and *Wuthering Heights* in the following
December. Charlotte, who had now made a literary
friendship with Mr. Williams, reader to her publishers,
Smith, Elder and Company, spoke of it on the eve of its
reception into the world as more vigorous and original
than her own production. Charlotte was shocked by
the power in it, the power of the "strong original mind"
behind it. "Ellis will improve, however," she added,
"because he knows his defects." Soon after these pub-
lications began that misattribution of authorship in the
press that caused Charlotte so much agitation. *The
Athenæum* and other papers attributed *Jane Eyre* to
Ellis Bell. "Ellis Bell is strong enough to stand without
being propped by Currer Bell," said Charlotte, obviously
nervous of appearing under that dark name.

By February 5th, 1848, *Wuthering Heights* began to sell.

Again Charlotte wrote of Ellis Bell to Mr. Williams.

"I should much—very much—like to take that quiet view of the 'great world' you allude to . . . Ellis, I imagine, would soon turn aside from the spectacle in disgust. I do not think he admits it as his creed that 'the proper study of mankind is man'—at least not the artificial man of cities. In some points I consider Ellis somewhat of a theorist: now and then he broaches ideas which strike my sense as much more daring and original than practical; his reason may be in advance of mine, but certainly it often travels a different road. I should say Ellis will not be seen in his full strength till he is seen as an essayist.

In March Charlotte was still worrying about the mistake of "authorship of *Wuthering Heights*." In September Mr. Newby had so far fostered the belief that one author had written all the Bell books that business complications arose over American publication. As far as I can make out, he took up the mistake made by the press and insinuated that Currer and Acton were both his client Ellis under different signatures. In July, 1848, Charlotte took Anne with her to London to clear the matter up and show that at least two Bells existed in the flesh. She explained that there was also another sister, Emily Jane, the Ellis of *Wuthering Heights*. When she returned and told Emily that she had disclosed her identity, Emily apparently was furious. "Permit me to caution you," wrote Charlotte to Mr. Williams, "not to speak of my sisters when you write to me. I mean, do not use the word in the plural. Ellis Bell will not endure to be alluded to under any other appellation than the *nom de plume*." Charlotte had regretted her disclosure directly she had made it. "I regret it bitterly now, for I find it is against every feeling and intention of Ellis Bell."

In August Charlotte drew an interesting comparison between Huntingdon, Rochester and Heathcliff for Mr. Williams, who evidently saw a likeness between the two former, and there comes that passage I have quoted beginning "Heathcliffe, again, of *Wuthering Heights* is quite another creation." Charlotte continued to be repulsed by that book, repulsed, and I feel fascinated. She tried to keep Heathcliff within the bounds of his own character, but had to admit that his spirit breathed through the whole narrative and haunted the whole scene.

Charlotte's disapprobation of Heathcliff and horror at the book fell a long way short, in words at least of what the press and public felt about it. Nevertheless, she did not want her work to appear as Ellis Bell's. Owing to an initial mistake of hers in which she persisted although she owned to it at the beginning, *Wuthering Heights* has always been said to have been attributed to Currer Bell. It was the other way about. *Jane Eyre* was attributed to Ellis, not *Wuthering Heights* to Currer Bell.

Not a word of all this business did Charlotte tell to Ellen Nussey. Although Ellen resumed her visits to

Haworth, now that Branwell had settled down to a career of vice, although Ellen Nussey had her suspicions, and communicated them, not a word concerning the Bells were spoken to her, and her suspicions were met with flat denial until the cat publicly leaped out of the bag. Charlotte continued her regular correspondence with her, but very few are her references therein to Emily. Ellen sent Emily some apples and a collar once by Charlotte. She smiled when Charlotte gave them to her "with an expression at once well pleased and slightly surprised." Only once more do we hear of Emily's smile. Very shortly before she died Charlotte read her a review of *Wuthering Heights* from *The North American Review* "Ellis, the 'man of uncommon talents, but dogged, brutal, and morose' . . . smiled half-amused and half in scorn as he listened."

Sometime in the late summer or autumn of 1848 Charlotte began another novel (*Shirley,* presumably) but the writing of this novel was interrupted by death. On September 24th Patrick Branwell Brontë died, aged thirty-one years. For some reason or another Branwell and Emily were thought to be a year younger than they really were, at the time of their deaths and Anne two years younger.

Many and bitter are the legends of Branwell's last years. It is said that Charlotte refused to speak to him and did not speak to him for long before he died, that he made Hell at night in the Parsonage, that his mania became homicidal. Many things are said. Whether Branwell perished of consumption or directly from the destructive powers of drink and drugs is not very clear to me. From Charlotte's letters it is quite clear however that he died in peace. For two days before his death his old self returned to him, "all the bitterness seemed gone," all his bitterness toward his relations was vanished away.

People say that at the end he fought death on his feet and died standing. It may very well be so.

"It is not permitted us to grieve for him who is gone as others grieve for those they lose," wrote Charlotte to Mr. Williams. ". . . I do not weep from a sense of bereavement, . . . but for the wreck of talent, the ruin of promise . . . ," but in time she mourned him in a better spirit. His sins were forgotten, his woes only remembered.

Of Emily's feelings toward her brother after his death I have spoken; but if her poem means anything it shows there was not much genuine regret in the Brontë family for Branwell's loss.

Emily caught a cold, at Branwell's funeral perhaps; she who hardly ever ailed fell slightly ill of an ordinary complaint. Emily's cold persisted. She began to cough. Charlotte began to feel she was seriously indisposed, but it was useless to question her about her state, she refused to answer, nor would she adopt any remedies suggested. A month passed, and Emily grew worse. She absolutely refused to admit that she was ill to anybody, and performed all the duties she was accustomed to perform as usual. "Emily," Charlotte told Mr. Williams, "has something like a slow inflammation of the lungs . . .

277

She is a real stoic in illness: she neither seeks nor will accept sympathy. To put any questions, to offer any aid, is to annoy. . . . The tie of sister is near and dear indeed, and I think a certain harshness in her powerful and peculiar character only makes me cling to her more. But this is all family egotism (so to speak)—excuse it, and, above all, never allude to it, or to the name Emily, when you write to me." Charlotte did not dare let Emily know she discussed her with other people.

Emily grew worse and worse. By the 16th of November her symptoms were more pronounced. Charlotte evidently took counsel with Mr. Williams about her, and he wrote a letter on the subject of homœopathic treatment of the case which she showed to Emily. Emily, whom no entreaty or reasoning could persuade to see a doctor, merely said, "Mr. Williams' intention was kind and good, but he was under a delusion: Homœopathy was only another form of quackery."

On November 23rd, Charlotte wrote to Ellen Nussey that Emily was very ill. She still resolutely refused to see a doctor; she would "not give an explanation of her feelings," she would "scarcely allow her illness to be alluded to." "I have been forced boldly to regard the terrible event of her loss as possible and even probable. . . . I think Emily seems the nearest thing to my heart in this world."

In another letter Charlotte told Ellen that she had mentioned a proposed visit of Ellen's to Emily, but "found however, it would not do; any, the slightest excitement or putting out of the way is not to be thought of . . . She is dear to me as life . . . She is too intractable. I *do* wish I knew her state and feelings more clearly."

Again to Mr. Williams Charlotte said, "I can give no favourable report of Emily's state. . . . My father shakes his head and speaks of others of our family once similarly afflicted. . . . Would that my sister added to her many great qualities the very humble one of tractability! I have again and again incurred her displeasure by urging the necessity of seeking advice, and I fear I must yet incur it again and again."

Emily slept alone during this illness. How she persisted in dying and dying alone by night and by day is terribly clear. Charlotte fought to penetrate that isolation as she had fought for nothing else in life. How she could fight has been made plain as daylight by her letters. Emily absolutely repulsed her. Not only her state of health but her state of mind she kept from those about her. Heathcliff had come to the time when he chose to depart from this world and no pity or love on earth could restrain him. He was gone all but the remnant of his body, days before Charlotte consulted Dr. Epps, a London physician, by letter. It was impossible to diagnose the case from Charlotte's description. Emily refused to take any interest in medical advice. She declared she would have "no poisoning doctor" near her. Dr. Epps sent some medicine for her, but she refused that too, refused everything until almost the last minute of her life. She refused assistance, sympathy or help of any kind, of all kinds. In the last hour of her life, she whispered, "If you will send for a doctor, I will see him now!" After that her will broke down and she could not help but show her frightful bodily sufferings; but at the last minute, at two o'clock in the afternoon when she was downstairs on the parlour sofa, while Charlotte and Anne begged her in agony to go to bed, she cried still, "No! No!" and tried to rise to her feet, but failed and fell back dead. So it is said.

"I cannot forget Emily's death-day; it becomes a more fixed, a darker, a more frequently recurring idea in my mind than ever. It was very terrible. She was torn, conscious, panting, reluctant, though resolute, out of a happy life. But it *will not do* to dwell on these things."

Was Emily torn reluctant out of a happy life? How did Catherine Earnshaw die?

"That wind. . . . Do let me feel it—it comes straight down the moor. Do let me have one breath! Open the window again wide: fasten it open!" Catherine Earnshaw let death in upon herself, let the cold wintry wind off the moor in upon her ailing body. How often Emily in those last days let the wind she had loved blow about her shoulders in the chill of a winter's night who can tell? Did Heathcliff, the Dark Hero, go down to the grave after his soul upon the wings of the wind?

Who knows?

> "Yes—I could swear that glorious wind
> Has swept the world aside,
> Has dashed its memory from thy mind
> Like foam-bells from the tide.

"And thou art now a spirit pouring
    Thy presence into all:
The essence of the tempest's roaring,
    And of the tempest's fall.

"A universal influence
    From thine own influence free;
A principal of life—intense—
    Lost to mortality."

APPENDIX I

The Brontës and Money

IN country districts like Haworth in the first half of last century almost everything was made at home. Bread, candles (tallow-dips), mats, mattresses, soap, jam, bacon, and many other things we now buy. Tea, sugar, and wax candles (very sparingly used at the Parsonage) were expensive; flour was still dear owing to the late European war; meat was comparatively expensive. Other necessities were cheap, and there were no luxuries used in the Brontë family beyond tea.

The Brontës lived rent-free. They kept two servants when they could get them whose joint wages were not likely to have exceeded £10 a year. Mr. Brontë allowed his old mother in Ireland £20 a year until she died and gave his Irish relatives "considerable sums." At one time apparently he was prepared to spend £60 a year on his daughters' education, the fees for four of them at Cowan Bridge.

Just at the time when Branwell, according to Charlotte, was embarrassing the family finances with his debts, the girls spent about £46 10s. on privately printing their poems and old Brontë went to Manchester for an operation and remained in lodgings for over a month with Charlotte, attended part of the time by a nurse and two doctors.

To show the scale of living in which the family indulged, I may remark that in 1836-37 Charlotte deplored that after clothing Anne and herself very little remained out of her wages of £16 per annum!

In 1849 Charlotte sent Ellen Nussey a £5 note and obtained for it one patent shower bath, one sable boa and cuffs, one squirrel ditto, and out of what remained told Ellen to buy something "to make your bride's-maid gear" for the wedding of a friend.

I cannot exactly arrive at what Mr. Brontë's total income was after his wife's death. It must have been about £250 a year. Aunt Branwell brought another £50 a year to the house out of which she saved a few hundred pounds in the course of her life. Anne and Branwell kept themselves for four years, roughly speaking. Charlotte, before she began to make money by writing, worked about the same length of time off and on.

Charlotte's dream of bliss was £200 a year, which she more or less realized after *Jane Eyre* was published. £1,000 per annum was absolute wealth in her eyes, and in my young days that sum was considered beyond question real riches. (See *Jane Eyre* and *Shirley*.)

Emily seems to have had higher notions. Till Aunt left her about £300, she was personally entirely destitute but for a few pounds earned at Miss Patchett's academy. Nothing short of an estate would have suited her. (See *Shirley* and *Wuthering Heights*.)

I doubt whether I am wrong in surmising that Mr. Brontë's household expenses averaged less than £160 in a twelvemonth. Out of this he entertained his daughters' friends and kept his children when they were at home. Between him and Miss Branwell their education was paid for, Branwell given some sort of an allowance and some sort of an education in art, the poor of Haworth were relieved, a curate probably in part maintained. Miss Branwell saved money.

One has always felt that the Brontës lived in straitened circumstances, but though unable to make a show of any kind, I do not believe there was any shortage or want at the Parsonage, except shortage of sleeping room. This affected only the girls. The house was bare, not through want of money, but because in a florid age the Brontës had simple old-fashioned furniture, and Mr. Brontë forbade curtains and other flummery. Charlotte's continuous craving for independence and Mrs. Gaskell's dramatic power have been responsible for the tradition of the Brontës' poverty, I think.

Living was incredibly low in Yorkshire even at the end of last century. Here are some of the prices I remember. Rent of four-

284

roomed cottage, eighteen-pence a week; gas to light same, one shilling a quarter; oranges, four a penny; herrings two a penny; cod, beneath contempt; ditto, legs of mutton; head housemaid's wages, five shillings a week; governess, ten shillings; "girl" aged fourteen, one shilling or nothing; best coal, less than one-third of the price of the worst now.

APPENDIX II

Death, Disease and the Brontës

Mrs. Patrick Brontë apparently died of cancer. Maria and Elizabeth Brontë died of the effects of malnutrition and cold following upon measles and whooping-cough, from which they were not really well when they went to Cowan Bridge, *i.e.*, "decline," congestion of the lungs, or consumption (?). Patrick Branwell Brontë died of some state of health aggravated or induced by depression, drink, and drugs. Francis Grundy refers to his "diseased genius," but what he means I cannot solve. Did he take drugs to combat pain? Was he consumptive? Emily Jane Brontë died of a neglected cold which developed into inflammation of the lungs. Except for an attack of erysipelas there is no record of her ever having ailed. Anne Brontë seems to have died of ordinary chronic tuberculosis, the only one of the family who did as far as I can tell.

Charlotte Brontë, like her father, seems to have suffered with her digestion. What she died of we do not know. It may have been from a fall from a horse, a bad neglected cold, or some chronic disorder of her organs. She was pregnant at the time of her death. Miss Elizabeth Branwell died of "internal obstruction" which is very likely to have developed into peritonitis. The Reverend Patrick Brontë died of old age.

"Decline" seems to have been a generic term for wasting diseases. I may point out that apart from any family tendency to tuberculosis, that disease was shockingly prevalent in the cold North of England in those days. Among the Brontës' friends, Ellen Nussey's sister "spat blood." Mary Taylor (who slept with one or more of the Brontë girls at the Parsonage) was thought to be about to die of it for some years. Ellen Nussey herself had fears of the same trouble. No isolation was practised; its infection was probably unknown. The extraordinary thing to me is, not that five of the Brontë children died of some lung trouble, but that three of them survived exposure to frequent infection and contagion for thirty years. If they were predisposed to tuberculosis, they must have had otherwise iron constitutions. I may add that influenza was the same curse of English winters that it is now.

Note that measles, "fever," and consumption are the diseases in *Wuthering Heights.* One may take "fever" to mean typhoid or one of its fellows, for it, not scarlet fever, was *the fever* par excellence in Haworth.

All the four Brontë children who survived to maturity were neurotic. Anne suffered from melancholia (religious variety). Charlotte at one time had an aggravated form of religious mania in which she nearly became insane through conviction of her own damnation. Mary Taylor ascribed her "depressions" to stomach disorder. Branwell suffered from genuine delusions apparently and abnormal conceit. Emily had what I believe is called persecution mania. Sense of inferiority, abnormal conceit gone the other way about, afflicted both Charlotte and Emily. In a sense Branwell and Emily were very mad and Charlotte intermittently mad. Neither old Brontë nor any of the children can have been comfortable domestic animals. Family good manners probably repressed many volcanic disturbances. There is evidence that Charlotte was sick and went off her food, Emily wept or turned deathly pale and stark with temper, Anne groused, and Branwell drank, all to relieve their feelings in those circumstances in which tradition says Mr. Brontë relieved his by pistol shooting.

APPENDIX III

Charlotte Brontë and Emily's Poems: A Surmise

IN 1850 Charlotte Brontë wrote: "One day, in the autumn of 1845, I accidentally lighted on a MS. volume of verse in my sister Emily's handwriting." This MS. volume is thought to be that now in the Honresfeld collection. The last poem in that book is *No coward soul is mine,* dated January 2nd, 1846. Almost all the poems of Ellis Bell published in 1846 are in this MS.

We know that Charlotte was very inaccurate with her dates. (See the Brontë memorial plaques in Haworth Church and Charlotte's references to Emily's age in the Preface to the Literary Remains. In these instances her errors in regard to Emily's age vary from one to three years.) It seems highly likely that the Honresfeld MS. with the *Last Lines* at the end of it fell complete into Charlotte's hands sometime after the New Year, 1846.

The discovery that they—Charlotte, Emily, and Anne—had written poems evidently led—probably Charlotte—to propose that they should each write a tale. I give the date February to May, 1846, as the probable time during which *The Professor, Wuthering Heights* and *Agnes Grey* were written.

It is now established fact that Charlotte "edited" Emily's poems. (See Mr. Davidson Cook's article in *The Nineteenth Century and After,* August, 1926.)

One gathers that after January, 1846, Emily, showed Charlotte no poems she afterwards wrote, but that some of them were found by Charlotte after her sister's death among her other papers. Otherwise the whole Preface to the Literary Remains is adjusted, as I am inclined to think, for public consumption.

Note that Emily wrote the figure 8 very like 3, and had I not seen *The Wanderer,* undoubtedly dated 1838, in which 8 is almost 3,

I might have less courageously decided, supported by Mr. Hatfield, that one at least of her poems dated 1843 hitherto belonged to 1848. Internal evidence seems to point to at least two poems belonging to the period after Charlotte's discovery, *i.e.*, *The Wanderer from the Fold*, probably written in October, 1848, inspired in all likelihood by Branwell's death, and *Why ask to know what date, what clime?* which I am inclined to date May (15th?), 1848, probably inspired by the Chartist disturbances in that month, when the Chartists were violently put down in Bradford and the district.

A previous poem, *It was the autumn of the year* (dated September 14th, 1846), which contains half of this latter poem in a slightly different version, has a Chartist smell about it too. Hitherto the riots in *Shirley* are supposed to have been founded on tales of the Luddite revolts which Charlotte heard at Roe Head, but the crematory glow in the valley represented in the last part of this poem suggests that the Brontës themselves witnessed at least the after effects of proletarian wrath. Charlotte began *Shirley* in 1848. When the movement of revolt came to a head and was in that district apparently suppressed, Shirley's interest therein was perhaps not all fiction.

I end with a question. Did Charlotte ever see all the poems of Emily Jane Brontë known to us?

APPENDIX IV

Emily Jane Brontë's Poems of Guilt

I GIVE here a list of Emily Jane Brontë's poems of guilt compiled from Clement Shorter's *Complete Poems of Emily Jane Brontë*, 1923:

April 28th, 1839, *Lines:* "*The soft unclouded blue of air.*" Page 105.

May 17th, 1839, "*I am the only being whose doom.*" Page 108.

July 26th, 1839, "*Shed no tears o'er that tomb.*" Page 116.

November 14th, 1839, *Stanzas to* —— : "*Well, some may hate, and some may scorn.*" Page 28.

January 6th, 1840, "*Thy sun is near meridian height.*" Page 128.

March, 1840, "*Far, far away is mirth withdrawn.*" Page 130.

March 27th, 1842 (?), "*What winter floods, what streams of spring.*" Page 141.

May 17th, 1842, "*In the same place, where nature wore.*" Page 142.

October 2nd, 1842, to February 2nd, 1843, *Self-Interrogation:* "*The evening passes fast away.*" Page 25.

March 2nd, 1844, "*This summer wind with thee and me.*" Page 159.

May, 1844, (A long collection of Gondal verse.) Page 160.

Undated (1844?), *Honour's Martyr.* Page 29.

Undated (1844?), "*All hushed and still within the house.*" Page 187.

These poems each contain references to crime, guilt, sin, shame, corruption, wrong, tarnished name or blighted fame, with the exception of the third which concerns entirely an "accursed man."

290

In addition to these thirteen poems, there are others which might be included in this list by some, for instance, *Aspin Castle, Death,* "*Still beside that dreary water,*" and a few more, but I have taken the minimum rather than the maximum number of poems of guilt, crime, blighted fame and damnation.

It is now known that there exist four cancelled lines of *The Philosopher* (see page 222) which ended that poem with these words: "The traitor's Deliverer, Death!" In spite therefore of the attitude Emily Brontë took up in *Honour's Martyr,* the philosopher evidently still considered himself a traitor.

With all this, and with Catherine's betrayal in *Wuthering Heights* to help me, I am no nearer the source of these poems of guilt. One has to feel that Emily betrayed, or thought she betrayed, some one she loved, but who or what her victim was, or if the whole thing was a morbid delusion, like Branwell's delusion over Mrs. Robinson, I cannot possibly say.

For those who wish to try their ingenuity by attempting to solve this riddle I suggest, as was suggested to me, the name Lovelace. See Richardson's *Clarissa* and the *Poems* of Richard Lovelace. Compare *Honour's Martyr* with *To Althea on Going to the Wars.* The name Lovelace seems to have had some significance for Emily. (Lovelace the betrayer and Lovelace who justified his desertion of Althea.) It is more than likely that Emily read Richardson's novels as Charlotte did, and there is internal evidence in Emily's poems that she studied the poems of the diviner Lovelace, probably led to do so by the name,

APPENDIX V

Wuthering Heights: The Place

I AM not going to say anything here about the exact situation of Wuthering Heights as determined by Brontë students or by tradition. Like most scenes in fiction, it is probably composite. Emmott Hall (see illustration) gives an excellent idea of the class of house Wuthering Heights itself was. Emmott Hall is to be seen near Haworth.

As for Thrushcross Grange, there are many houses of that kind to be found in the north. The name Thruscross exists as the name of a small hamlet on the tract of moor to the north of Bradford. Within walking distance is a spot called Heathfield.

The Penistone Crags which lay "about a mile and a half beyond Mr. Heathcliff's place," have been traditionally confused with the Penistone Crags above Penistone near Sheffield, but there is a spot called by the name Penistone on the moors just up behind Haworth, and this is probably the place Emily Brontë had in mind.